Professional Email Writing & Etiquette Write Better Emails

SADANAND PUJARI

Published by SADANAND PUJARI, 2023.

Table of Contents

Copyright 1

About 2

Book Overview 3

Introduction 7

Using Email to Build Your Reputation 10

Using Email for Group Updates 16

Using Email for Collaboration 22

Using Email for Recordkeeping 26

Section Two 30

Building and Improving Relationships Through Emails 33

Using Humor in Business Emails 39

Building Credibility In Business Emails 43

Modifying Emails to Cope with Cultural Nuances 48

Email Communication Across the Generational Gap 53

Section Three 58

How to Write Effective Subject Lines 61

Why Should You Focus On Your Greetings 65

Writing the Main Content 70

Providing Supporting Information 74

Using the Right Sign-offs And Signatures 80

Section Four 84

How to Compose Clear Email Messages 88

Writing and Organizing Long Emails 93

Proofreading and Editing Your Work 99

Common Grammar Mistakes in Business Emails 104

Common Punctuation Mistakes 110

Tools for Checking Grammar and Punctuation 114

Copyright

Copyright © 2023 by **SADANAND PUJARI**

All rights reserved. No part of this book may be reproduced, scanned, or distributed in any printed or electronic form without permission. Please do not participate in or encourage piracy of copyrighted materials in violation of the author's rights. Purchase only authorized editions.

Professional Email Writing & Etiquette Write Better Emails

First Edition: Dec 2023

Book Design by **SADANAND PUJARI**

About

Unlock your full potential in email communication with our comprehensive and cutting-edge Book: Professional Email Writing & Etiquette - Write Better Emails. Transform your emails into powerful, engaging, and polished messages that command attention and leave a lasting impression.

This immersive Book offers a deep dive into every aspect of professional email writing, covering everything from email etiquette and style to mastering the power of ChatGPT AI for enhancing your email writing skills. We've designed this Book to help you become a confident and effective communicator, setting you apart in your personal and professional life.

Our Professional Email Writing & Etiquette - Write Better Emails Book is designed for professionals, entrepreneurs, students, job seekers, and anyone looking to enhance their email communication skills. With expert guidance, engaging content, and practical examples, you'll quickly transform your emails into compelling tools for success.

The Book is technology-agnostic. This means that it doesn't matter which email technology tool you use (Gmail, Outlook, Yahoo, etc).

Don't miss this opportunity to elevate your email writing skills to new heights. Enroll now and become an email communication pro with Professional Email Writing & Etiquette - Write Better Emails.

Book Overview

Hi, thank you for enrolling. I'm happy to see you decided to join, enrolling in this Book demonstrates that you are actively engaged in learning and are serious about professional development. Email writing skills are highly valued in business communication, and they play a significant role in your daily interactions with your colleagues. By building and improving your email writing skills, you will gain more confidence, enhance your professional reputation and grow your career.

Welcome. I'm Victoria. I'll be your instructor for this Book. I work as a director of Marketing Student Support, a Corporate Finance Institute. CFI is the world's leading financial training provider, with over 700,000 students and thousands of five star reviews. By serving over half a million customers and managing two busy teams, I gained hands-on experience and email writing skills to help me effectively manage projects, communicate with colleagues and grow professionally. But that's just an example.

This Book is all about you. My goal is to share everything I know about email communication to help you learn, grow and achieve your goals, unlike many other Books that share little bits and pieces. This Book is designed to give you a comprehensive training on email writing and email etiquette at work. It goes beyond theory and provides easy to implement example's scripts and advice that you can start applying as soon as you read the chapters. This Book is for you if you want to build your professional reputation and enhance your career success using email communication. The Book starts with the basics and how to maximize email potential in business communication.

We'll look at what role IMOS play in building your professional reputation, how to use them for group wide updates, team collaboration and record keeping. In chapter two, the focus will be on building and improving relationships through business emails. We'll discuss how to use humor in business emails and when it is appropriate. To do so. You'll learn how to use emails to build credibility, modify your emails to cope with cultural differences, and expand your knowledge of email communication across the generational gap. In chapter three, we'll cover the core elements of email writing. I'll show you how to write effective subject lines for your emails.

We'll take a close look at email greetings and want to keep in mind when writing the main body, then you learn about providing supporting information in the form of facts, documents, screenshots, attachments and using the right sign offs and signatures. In chapter four, I'll share tips on how to write clear email messages. I'll provide you with examples showing you how to make long and complex emails scannable and straightforward for your recipients. You'll also learn about proofreading and editing your emails to make them clear, concise and easy to understand will also cover common grammar and punctuation mistakes made in business emails and how to fix them.

We'll also go through a list of recommended tools for checking grammar and punctuation in your writing. chapter five covers etiquette about the built -in email features you will learn how to use to seek Bekesi reply and reply to all fields correctly. Then we're going to look at proper ways you can forward emails without annoying your recipients. You'll also learn about email, attachment etiquette and how to create effective email templates to manage repetitive emails and save time. And finally, in the chapter, you'll also learn about etiquette about built-In email features. In chapter six, we'll talk about coping with common email communication challenges. For example, how to get colleagues to respond to your emails, how to say no without creating tension at work, how to respond to confusing emails. You'll also learn how to respond to rude and passive aggressive emails in the chapter.

chapter seven discusses emails for everyday workplace situations such as writing introduction and follow up emails, how to delegate tasks and discuss meetings and events. You learn how to reschedule, cancel and invite someone to a meeting using email. I'll also share tips on how to write impactful appreciation and congratulations emails, as well as delivering good and bad news using email. Then we'll look at how to request vacations, announce absences, sick leaves and how to report workplace issues as well as discuss solutions. Using email. We'll end the chapter by talking about the importance of apology emails and how to write them. In chapter eight, I'd like to answer a few common questions regarding challenging situations at work and how to address them through emails. These will give you some insights and ideas on how to handle various workplace situations. At the end of the Book, I added a complimentary chapter about covid-19 and how this has affected email communication and what key considerations to keep in mind while writing emails during the epidemic.

As you can see, we have lots of exciting content to cover in this Book. Remember that the best way to get the most out of online learning is to read the chapters, do the exercises and apply what you're learning in your daily communication. Feel free to post your questions in their chapter on your dashboard or message me directly. I'd love to hear from you. If you're ready to learn and expand your knowledge, let's get started and take your email communication skills to the next level.

Introduction

Because employers have so many different uses and benefits, there are various ways in which their potential can be realized, but their potential and business communication can only be maximized if both the company and individual employees are on board together. This chapter is designed to help you understand how the true potential of emails and business communication can be achieved. Emails can be used in a wide variety of ways, even if you set aside all their benefits and sales and marketing and focus solely on internal business communication.

Email still has many users, but all their benefits are only theoretical in nature until they're put into practice, maximizing email potential and business communication in simple words. It's not always a fast and easy task. It is an ongoing goal that requires time and effort from both the company and its employees. In fact, to make the most of email communication for business success, you need things to work at two different levels. The first level, you need the company to be committed to the idea that it would result in appropriate policy decisions and guidelines. And the second level, you need individual professionals to put an effort into maximizing their use of emails in the best way possible.

Companies need to look at various ways in which they can maximize email potential within their internal and external communication channels. It is also their role to guide professionals on doing the same independently to make this happen. This chapter contains four different chapters, with each one focusing on one key way through which email potential can be maximized in business communication. Let's take a look at what we're going to cover in the first chapter. We'll look at ways you can use email to build your reputation in business. Companies and professionals thrive equally on their reputation. Your reputation is important for your career success, growth, networking and team collaboration. One of the things that affects your reputation is how professional your email communication is.

Unprofessional emails will have a negative effect on both individual's reputation directly and the company they work for. In this chapter, focus on what your professional emails look like, and how you can improve your reputation, ensuring that your emails have a positive impression on your recipients. And the second chapter will look at ways email can be used for group wide updates. Emails excel when used for group updates, but only if they're used in a uniform and standardized manner. This means that companies need to make key policy decisions and create procedures for the team to follow. In this chapter, I will describe the three most common types of group rate updates and show you how email should be used for each one. In the third chapter I will look at ways how email is used for team collaboration. Emails can be very beneficial when used for collaboration between employees, team members and departments.

In this chapter, I first explain how emails when used for collaboration can result in numerous wide ranging benefits in the second half. I don't dip into the most important of these benefits. And in the fourth chapter, we'll take a look at how emails can be used for record keeping. Emails may not be designed for record keeping, but they in fact are very useful for such purposes because of various built in features and tools. In this chapter, I talk about why and how emails are great for record keeping in business while focusing on individual aspects such as ease of use, storage, archiving and accessibility. So if you're ready to continue learning, I'll see you in the next chapter.

Using Email to Build Your Reputation

Using email to build your reputation, professionalism at work translates directly to professionalism in email, communication and vice versa. When an individual's email is unprofessional, it can result in the recipient thinking that the sender is unprofessional, which affects the center's reputation to prevent a negative reputation. You need to write your email as well. And to do this you need to know what professional emails look like.

This chapter will help you with each of these aspects. In this chapter, we will cover the connection between email, writing, professionalism and reputation, understanding your target audience, the relevance of cultural considerations in international business emails, and the impact of email errors on your reputation. There is a direct connection between email communication and your professional reputation. Some people may discount the importance of email communication at work. This is understandable because the connection is very subtle. Let me explain the relationship between email, writing, professionalism and reputation. Professionalism is very important to the business community because it signifies responsibility, respect, accuracy and your growth potential.

Externally, companies need their employees to be professional in their email communication because they are representing the business internally. They need their employees to be professional, to create an efficient work environment so a person's professionalism becomes critical to his or her overall reputation and career success. All this emphasis on professionalism applies to emails to one individual who takes email writing casually. The emails they create have inherent flaws, and when recipients read these poorly written emails, their opinion of the sender changes for the worse. These flaws can be of various types, ranging from typos and incomplete information to the use of improper words or tones. But the impression they create is universal. They make the recipient think that the sender lacks professionalism and as a result, the individual's reputation plummets, or the recipient thinking that the sender lacks knowledge or attention to detail.

The obvious question at this point is what can you do to prevent this from happening to you? The simple answer is to write professional emails, but that's easier said than done. In practice, it isn't so easy. Without knowing how to define professional emails, the rest of this chapter will help you recognize high quality emails at work and ensure that you can meet those standards. You'll need to keep this in mind that a professional email is written to suit the target audience. Communication is all about the target audience. It doesn't matter whether you're in a conference call or whether you're writing a letter. Your target audience should define the words he used as well as the tone you take.

A good example of this would be how the writing style and choice of words change between an email being sent to a client and one being sent to associates or subordinates, even when the basic content is about the same. Here's an example of this one. If you're writing an apology to a client, you might say we apologize for the delay in the completion of this project. We estimate that it should be completed by October 15th thousand twenty two. If you are emailing your team, you might say, I'm sorry, but it looks like this project is going to be late. I think we may be able to finish by the 15th of this month the key differences in both the words being used and the tone of the communication being taken, the words apologize and completed are much more formal and suitable to a client than sorry and finish. Similarly, the format of the date is different in both.

Knowing and understanding your audience is key to effective email writing when preparing to write your email, the first question to ask is who am I writing this for? Knowing who your sender is means that you adapt your tone and content of your writing to suit your audience. Professional emails are not written casually. Instead, they're very well considered with the writing, putting a lot of thought into individual words and their context. This is especially evident in international or intercultural communication when writing to someone from another country or culture. Next, I'd like to talk about cultural mistakes in email communication. Let's look at some examples of how cultural differences can affect your email communication. The definition of formal tone varies from one country to another. For example, for Americans and Australians, it's not uncommon to be more informal than for people from other countries. This business outlook is very different from the business outlook of people with other nationalities.

The result is they might open their email with more casual greetings, such as Hi Adam, or end it with cheers. But if the recipient is in Saudi Arabia or Japan, the same greeting a sign off might be considered too friendly or even offensive for some people in business communication. Here's another example. In Germany, people write the main body of their emails differently in comparison to North America and other countries. They prefer not to capitalize the first sentence in the paragraph after the greeting. Here's an example. Here's how we do it in North America. As you can see in this example, we capitalize the first sentence after the greeting, dorsum regarding the project being discussed, I would like to add. But in Germany, people would not capitalize the R in the beginning of the paragraph dorsum regarding the project being discussed, I would like to add, as you can see in the second example in Germany, it is acceptable not to capitalize the first sentence after the greeting.

Titles are also something you need to be careful about, and cross-cultural, IMO, is a good example of this is seen with Middle Eastern countries such as Saudi Arabia. Saudi Arabia is ruled by the royal family and the royal family is big with lots of members. Many of them have specific titles such as Your Highness and Your Excellency. In your email, you not only have to use these titles appropriately, but repeatedly. In fact, you have to avoid directly addressing the recipient and use these titles instead. As you can see, you need to be careful when choosing your language of business communication, especially when you're working in a multicultural setting or dealing with international clients. These are just a few examples to illustrate some differences when it comes to email communication. But the main point is that you need to be aware that cultural differences do exist in business writing and they need to be considered when writing your emails.

Professional emails are also free of grammatical errors, errors can appear in various forms and email writing No. One, they can be vocabulary based with similar sounding words being confused by the writer. Here are some common examples of these types of words. Affect and effect. Accept and accept then and then you're and you're here and here and so on, if you're typing in a hurry or using your phone and auto correct to type your message, take an extra minute, review what you wrote to make sure that you're not making any of these mistakes. Errors can also be simple spelling mistakes caused because of negligence or lack of time on the part of the writer. For example, let's say you wanted to write the word reciprocate. Here's what it looks like with a spelling mistake.

While the correct spelling should be like this, or some people might have been right and text speaks such as what do you want to do in place of what do you want to do? Although common in text messaging, it wouldn't be appropriate in business communication, and then there could be punctuation based mistakes as well. Let's take a look at some examples using let's eat fins in place of let's eat comma events or using too many punctuations such as happy to hear from you with many exclamation marks. That's an excessive amount of claymation work or capitalization. That's another common mistake.

For example, using good to hear from you when it should be good to hear from you with a capital G, you need to pay close attention to your email to make sure you aren't making any of these mistakes and set aside some time to review and edit what you wrote. Check the vocabulary, spelling and grammar to make sure your emails are sound polished and professional. In summary, people often translate lack of professionalism in business communication, not only to the individual being entirely unprofessional, but also to the company being unprofessional in the services. This is why the way you write an email can have a huge impact on your reputation. Demonstrating professionalism in emails is about knowing what a professional email looks like and being alert when writing them.

Using Email for Group Updates

Emails can excel in various types of groups and updates, but the way they are used needs to be governed by a structure that individuals need to follow and managers need to establish. Putting such a structure in place will not only help managers create a coherent work culture, but it will also minimize confusion and help professionals ensure efficient communication at work. The goal is to create emails that are logical and easy to understand.

This chapter is designed to outline such a structure for both managers and employees in this chapter, which will cover three types of group wide updates that emails excel at a step by step process for using emails, for group wide updates, for managers and individual professionals, creating relevant email groups, learning or training the workforce on the email platform, and following or establishing email templates and guidelines. In-house communication has always been important in business to ensure all employees and departments coordinate and pull the business in a unified direction. But before emails came and changed the business communication landscape, companies used traditional memos to share information internally. In fact, before the arrival of email, businesses would avoid system wide in-house modifications and policy changes because it was expensive. Similarly, employees would avoid in-house communications because initiating new memos was time consuming and effort intensive.

This kind of aversion to in-house business communication can appear even with emails unless employees, teams and departments as well as their managers learn how to use emails from the perspective of group wide updates. To do this, the first step is to understand what kind of group updates emails can be used for. This is why I will begin this chapter with these three main types of group wide updates before moving on to the intricacies of using emails in this way. So let's go ahead and look at the three types of group wide updates that you most excel at. All the reasons why companies need to use memos, apply to emails to the difference between old school memos and the morning email is that emails offer much more as tools for group wide in-house updates.

The reasons for this range from financial to environmental benefits to ease of use. So which types of group updates are most excellent? For the first and most important are operational updates. These are updates that actively affect the ongoing operations in a company in terms of deliverables and participants alike. Here are two examples of what kinds of operational updates emails can be used for. One example is meetings. Emails can be used for scheduling and rescheduling meetings, along with inviting, adding and removing individual participants. This becomes even easier with specific software and apps that automatically send emails on behalf of the organizer. Google Calendar integrated within Gmail, performs this task particularly well. Another example is project management.

Emails can be used for project management, while specialized project management tools exist. Most of them make use of emails in one form or another. Email is going to be used to update relevant parties about deadline changes, delays, tactical modifications, team formulations and even client negotiations. Ideally, systemic policy changes need to be announced simultaneously to all relevant individuals in a business to prevent mistakes and confusions and emails are particularly excellent at it. They can deliver important policy announcements to employees regardless of geographical or timezone related limitations.

A few different types of systemic policy announcement emails can be used to make our number one technical upgrades if the business is introducing a new app to the existing software ecosystem or the existing digital infrastructure is going to be inaccessible during maintenance, going can be used to inform all employees simultaneously. No two emails can also be used for H.R. policy changes or announcements. If management decides to modify the existing H.R. policies or append new rules and guidelines to it, then the workforce can be informed of all the changes to prevent indiscretions or problems arising through them. In the business world, it is a big win if management can get the workforce to be passionate about the company and the brand. This kind of involvement is best achieved by getting employees to invest in the business of success. Immelt can make this happen by supplying regular updates to the workforce about the business. Here are some examples.

One introduction. When new team members and employees are added to the workplace, emails can be used to introduce them to the existing staff and speed up their integration. No.

Two achievements. Everyone likes to feel like they've contributed to their work. So a business that communicates its great achievements with its staff through emails can benefit greatly by the employees deriving a sense of accomplishment and entertainment. Some businesses like to keep their employees interested and engaged by offering regular newsletters containing information that ranges from team building activities to standard updates about their personal achievements. Emails provide more flexible control over information being shared to larger in-house groups of employees than memos ever did. But this is only possible when they're used properly for making these announcements. So how do you go about using email for group rate updates, whether you're an employee using email to announce information to your associates or a manager looking to use emails to communicate with your team, the risk of making mistakes can be high even if you don't end up embarrassing yourself.

You still need to know how to use emails to make announcements to get the most out of them. This chapter will give you a quick roadmap to follow for this desk. One strategy for group wide updates could be creating relevant email groups. Sending an email to the wrong individuals could be pretty embarrassing. It's especially uncomfortable if you send an email to a large number of wrong individuals. This is where email groups come into the picture. The first step to using emails for making group updates is to create relevant email groups. If you group individuals based on shared responsibilities, then you've created a relevant email group. Here are some examples.

Example one, an email group containing email addresses of all the people working on the same project as you. These could be internal and external contacts who are working together, for example, to an email group with email addresses of all the people with the same responsibility. For example, if you want to email everyone to the marketing department, instead of adding their email addresses one by one, you can save time by email. The group you've already created with relevant email groups and place individuals, teams and departments will find it easier to communicate collectively provided that they're familiar with the email platform. Learning or training work for us on the email platform is crucial for strong communication at work. It is important to know how to use the email platform too, especially since different businesses use the platforms in a different way.

While email is the most popular platform today, some businesses use Microsoft Outlook or even third party service providers. Knowing how the email platform works is critical not only because it saves a lot of time, but also because it prevents mistakes. After you read the Book, make sure you take the time to explore all of the features we talk about throughout the Book using your email platform. The next thing we need to do to maximize the potential of group wide updates is to follow the established email templates and guidelines. If you are in a managerial position, then you need to make sure that such templates and guidelines are in place for your workforce. The purpose of the email templates is to standardize the format for various types of announcements and updates.

The purpose of the guidelines is to give the senders a rulebook that contains all of the email etiquettes the company expects from them. Together, the templates in the guidelines will ensure clarity, professionalism and coherence in how the company communicates internally. In summary, when used in-house for any type of group it updates, emails can be very useful, provided they are bound by certain rules and regulations for managers. This structure creates coherence in the company's internal communications and for professionals, such structures prevent conflicts and increase cooperation. To create such a system, you need to create relevant email groups, learn how to use available platforms and establish sufficient guidelines for team communication.

Using Email for Collaboration

One of the easiest ways of maximizing the potential of email and business communication is to focus on collaboration. The benefits of focusing on email collaboration between individual employees, departments and teams are vast. They affect every aspect of business and business communication. And in this chapter, we will explore how email collaboration is vital to the email platform, as well as how it can prove to be a game changer for a business. Here's what you're going to learn in this chapter using email collaboration to maximize the potential of the email platform. How email collaboration boosts productivity, avoiding confusion within a team through better email collaboration and creating a common identity and community through email collaboration.

Collaboration is huge and business employees know it. Employers know it and clients know it. In fact, multiple studies have proven the importance of collaboration in business from multiple angles. The broadest study was conducted at the Queen's University of Charlotte, where researchers at the university found that 75 percent of employers think that collaboration and teamwork are very important. This study is backed up by another conducted by Salesforce. This study found that more than 85 percent of surveyed employees and executives find a lack of collaboration and communication to be the primary reason for workplace failures, since email is the most commonly used medium for communication today. It is obvious that maximizing email potential as a collaboration tool is key to improve performance.

The study's hint that email collaboration is one of the ways of maximizing email potential in business communication. But they don't reveal how in this chapter we'll look at the how by analyzing the various benefits of email, collaboration and business. First of all, email collaboration improves productivity. Collaboration using email will have a direct impact on productivity, but the impact will come from two different directions. The first is that it improves speed and response time. It's easy to see how email collaboration can make a company more agile in terms of time. Emails offer instantaneous communication even when the message being conveyed is complex. This is especially true since mobile devices became accessible to everyone. Now people can check their emails even when they are not at their desks. Even geographic and time zone. Restrictive limitations have become redundant. Emails are also faster in terms of discussions. They allow team members to be quicker and more mentally adaptable, particularly when compared to conferences and meetings. They make it possible for the entire team to discuss the same subjects without moving away from their desks or even interrupting the work that they're currently doing.

The second way that email collaboration improves productivity is by boosting individual and collective performance. A study conducted by researchers at Stanford found that if the team members feel that they're collaborating, their performance gets supercharged. According to the findings of the study, collaborating employees are likely to work 60 percent more than others, which leads directly to improved performance. Apart from boosting response time and performance levels, more collaboration naturally also improves coordination between team members. In fact, coordination is the key to the entire thing and shouldn't be taken lightly, according to research by the MIT Sloan School of Management. Ninety seven percent of senior executives and employees think that they should have a clear understanding of the company's priorities, but only about 25 percent of them can accurately list them. This is precisely where IMO collaboration can make a difference, says IMOS, are free and instantaneous. They prevent confusion and allow team members to be consistently in touch with each other, aligning and realigning their goals, objectives, deadlines and tasks. They allow tasks to be delegated easily and transparently, which creates confidence and trust in everyone. IMO, collaboration also fosters a common team identity. The confidence and trust created through email collaboration directly leads to a strong sense of community.

The team members get a sense of belonging and feel that they're contributing even more. The teams themselves believe that they belong to the business and are making important contributions. All of this combined improves the morale and work culture of the business. The sense of community has its own set of benefits. The most important of these is the reduction of the number of employees leaving the company and a significant boost in talent retention again. Studies have been conducted to prove this fact. One study found that 54 percent of employees stay at a company longer than they wanted to purely because of the sense of community they had with their colleagues. There are two ways through which a business can focus on email collaboration. The first is directly through the email platform, and the second is through third party services and apps that are compatible with the email platforms being used to.

Examples of these are project management services, Asana and Trello. Trello is compatible with emails and allows for basic notifications, and Asthana allows for features and work management directly from the email notifications. If you are using your own email platform. Your goal should be to keep your email communication as uniform and efficient as possible. To achieve this employee, you should follow a similar email, reading an email and managing practices. It also means that the business has to create guidelines and policies for governing, email, collaboration and communication that all the staff can follow. With the second method, the compatibility between the third party service and the email platform being used by the company is crucial. While most third party services will offer some level of compatibility, the deeper the overlap, the better the collaboration will be within the team.

Focusing on email collaboration is one of the ways to which employees and employers can maximize the potential of the email platform altogether. Doing so will directly lead to significant jumps and performance levels. Productivity, response, time coordination, teamwork and talent retention.

Using Email for Recordkeeping

While they weren't initially built that way, you must have evolved to become inherently perfect for record keeping, they're now almost tailor made to make record keeping easier, faster, cheaper and more intuitive, even though most elements that make it most perfect for record keeping are not hidden. It still takes a shift in perspective to view them in that light. In this chapter, we will look at the nuances of these elements that make Imal such a great tool for archiving, filing and categorizing information.

Here's what you're going to learn in this chapter. How IMOS are suited to recordkeeping, storage concerns and using emails for record keeping, archiving, filing and categorizing information in emails and accessibility of archived information emails in the earlier years. Emails don't have the kind of features and capabilities the most email platforms have today. The simple design only allowed for simple messages to be sent from one person to another. Everything else was absent, ranging from the ability to send a single email to multiple people simultaneously to attaching files for greater clarity. But even though emails were not developed for record keeping purposes over the years, they have evolved in a way that makes them ideal for it. In fact, the way emails are used now in business makes them almost tailor made for recordkeeping.

Since nowadays emails are so naturally suited to categorizing and archiving information, this becomes one of the most important ways of maximizing their potential. To do this, though, it is important to understand why and how they're used for archiving, filing and storing information. In this chapter, we're going to explore this quality of emails. According to a recent Emulsifier six report, there were three point nine billion active email users in 2019. This was more than all the social media users in the world, which is three point five billion. The same report says that the number of email users is expected to grow by four percent every year for the next four years. This means that there will be more than four billion active email users in 2020 and about four point three billion active users by 2023.

The number of active email users is constantly growing because of how easy it is to get an email account. This is highlighted by the fact that emails are free. The reason why emails are so popular is also one of the reasons why there is such a great option for record keeping in business. In fact, regardless of which other methods of recordkeeping you compare emails to, they will always come out ahead in terms of cost. This is especially true when it comes to scalability. The storage capacity of most email accounts can be easily expanded at fairly low prices. Further, if a company has its own server, then the cost becomes fairly insignificant. IMO, suitability for recordkeeping isn't just about cost, though. It is also about intuitiveness. In email, the information that sits there until the user archives or deletes the file is automatically saved and stored unless it's consciously and actively removed.

IMO, platforms offer multiple built in features exclusively designed towards segmentation, these features are extremely easy to use when it comes to categorizing and archiving information. First, there are labels. Users can make as many labels as required to categorize all the incoming emails. This means an individual can label emails in terms of departments, clients and even projects as shown in this example. Another common feature that boosts the recordkeeping abilities of emails is filters. Filters are instructions to the email platform to send an email to a certain category automatically based on various conditions such as keywords and senders. Let's look at some examples. You can set up your email filters. So first I'll email sent by John Smith will be labeled and archived into Project A.B.C.. Second, all emails, including keyword salaries, will go to appraisals. And third, all emails mentioning the balance sheet will go to finance. I'm going to add some helpful resources to this chapter so you can follow the tutorials on how to set up filters. If you're not already familiar with this email feature.

All the shows that email platforms are equipped for archiving and filing purposes. Emails are also easy and quick to access, with mobile devices being commonly used and even offline is becoming possible. Accessing the archived emails is very convenient. One method is to look for emails through their folders or labels. For example, you click on a folder and it shows you all the emails it contains. This, as simple as it sounds, is the more roundabout method. The simpler method is to simply use the search function the same way that one uses the search engine, put in the records, hit search and you'll get all the relevant results. The more accurate your search, the quicker you get the email message you're looking for. This means that you'll no longer have to manually go through hundreds of files, digital or otherwise, to find the ones you're looking for. As a result, accessing archive files becomes not only easier, but also faster.

In summary, you also become increasingly more suitable for recordkeeping purposes in the modern age. They offer a lot of benefits that make them ideal for recordkeeping, such as storage space, built in labeling and filtering features and even inherent tools designed to make information more accessible, such as the search field. I'll see you in the next chapter.

Section Two

Any kind of communication will automatically result in the creation of a relationship. Similarly, if you already have a business relationship, then every discussion of correspondence you have will affect it in one way or another. The kind of relationship your emails help you form or whether they take your existing relationships is entirely up to you. The purpose of the chapter is to help you use your business emails to build and nurture your relationships at work. The moment the channels of communication are opened, a relationship is formed.

Even if the relationship is an extremely basic one between a sender and a receiver who don't know each other. A relationship is still formed when the communication starts. So, technically speaking, by the act of writing and sending an email, you're already started building a relationship. This means that the emails you send have an impact on the business relationships you create and how they develop. What if you could use your emails to improve the quality of your relationship with your colleagues? You wouldn't even matter whether you're trying to create a new relationship or evolve an already existing one into something better.

In this chapter, I will explain how you can use your emails to do exactly that. Here are all the chapters you find in the chapter and an overview of what each one is going to cover. In the chapter, one will look at creating new relationships and improving existing ones through emails. Certain factors play a role in how effective your emails are going to be when it comes to nurturing relationships in the first chapter. I'll focus on the most important of these factors, such as your tone, your writing style, whether you provide context or not, and how close you should stick to the established workplace hierarchies. I'll also describe how each factor impacts the potential of your email and what you can do to strengthen your message and build relationships that work and chapter to you. Learn how to use humor in business emails.

Now, whether humor should be used in business emails or not is a much debated subject. Usually the debate runs between the risks and the rewards connected to using humor in business emails. We're going to look at the pros and cons to help you make an informed decision. When writing your emails, you'll also learn how humor can make or break business relationships. And then we'll cover what you should or you shouldn't be doing when you're incorporating humor into your emails and chapter three. We'll look at how to build credibility in business emails. Credibility plays an essential role in the development of all relationships. Without credibility, no relationship will stand the test of time or any kind of pressure. In this chapter, I'll help you discover the importance of credibility in a relationship and how it can be fostered through subtle techniques and methods using email.

Next, a chapter for we'll look at modifying your emotions to cope with cultural differences is the proven fact that cultural differences play a major role in defining business. Relationships were not taken into account in emails. These differences can cause considerable miscommunication between the parties involved. This is why I've created this chapter. You learn what a professional should keep in mind when it comes to emailing business contacts across cultural and geographical boundaries. And finally, in chapter five, we'll talk about email communication across the generational gap.

People from different generations have different expectations and behavioral tendencies, which are informed by their unique experiences. As a result, generational gaps can be as significant as cultural differences in this chapter. We'll explore how the modern workplace incorporates more generations than ever before and how this affects email. Communication will then cover various ways in which you can bridge these generational gaps and build strong and healthy relationships at work. Are you ready to begin? I'll see you in the next chapter.

Building and Improving Relationships Through Emails

Immelt is an important channel of communication, like all types of communication, it is possible to use Immelt to create new relationships and improve existing ones through emails. It is all about knowing how to add personality and balancing the divide between formality and casualness in this chapter. I will explain exactly how you can go about doing this. Here's what you're going to learn. Using email to build business relationships.

How the tone of your emails can affect your professional relationships while providing context is critical and emails and learning how to move beyond hierarchy and restrictions. Communication has an impact on relationships. It doesn't matter what type of communication it is for or what channel you're using to communicate. As long as you're communicating, your relationship is evolving. If you're communicating for the first time ever, then you're creating new relationships. If you've been communicating with someone for some time, then you're either maintaining the status quo in your relationship or improving it. These are simple facts. Email is a suitable medium for creating new relationships and maintaining existing ones.

In fact, emails can be quite effective in forming bonds and persuading people toward a specific direction, provided they're used in the right manner and at the right time. In this chapter, I will be explaining how you can use emails to create new relationships and how we can use them to maintain and improve your existing ones. Now let's take a look at the style and tone of writing. It is possible that some people don't consider emails as a tool for building relationships because they think it's too impersonal or official. It's also possible that some people might think that emails are not suitable for building or maintaining relationships because they feel too casual. In other words, some people might think that emails are not suitable for building and maintaining relationships because they're either too formal or they're too informal. These two extremes hint at how email can be used to boost your relationships. If the email you're right is neither formal nor informal and is balanced in the middle, it becomes suitable for managing business relationships.

It's also about being professional without being detached and being friendly without seeming too artificial. Another way to look at it would be that it is about striking a balance between generic and personable. This balance, though, is quite subjective. In fact, this balance will change from one employer to another. The real marker of this balance is linked with the person you're sending the email to. You'll not only have to assess your relationship with the receiver, but also their personality. For instance, if you have a formal relationship with your boss, it would be inappropriate to send a cartoon or a joke. However, if you're sending an email to a colleague and you two have a close working relationship, a more informal type of content would be fine in the situation.

Similarly, you can't set an overly casual email to a client because you need to establish credibility and professionalism first. If you're emailing customers, you can still take a friendly tone provided that it doesn't clash with your company's communication strategy. Here's an important tip. Always provide context. Context is very important when it comes to emails because it keeps the conversation flowing and the recipient interested. In contrast, abruptness is a major obstacle in interpersonal relationships, irrespective of whether it's perceived texturally or face to face. Imagine yourself walking up to a colleague first thing in the morning and telling them how your new client makes you feel without first telling them about the new client or the news project.

Without context, they would be pretty confused. Or imagine walking up to someone you don't even know on the street and pitching them with an investment idea. And in both scenarios, your relationship will suffer without providing context. First, you'll make the colleague think that you're detached, socially inept or only concerned about work. This might result in the colleague taking a figurative step back from you that will have a negative effect on your working relationship. In the case of the new person on the street, you won't have a relationship at all. That person will not entertain your sales pitch and will probably be indifferent enough to just walk away. The same kind of thing happens in emails. You're just not there to see it. The colleague takes a backward step mentally and emotionally when the new person simply deletes the email. This is why context is everything when it comes to creating or maintaining relationships via email.

This means that if you're emailing a colleague, you need to start with something familiar and then provide them with some context so they clearly understand your objective. Let's take a look at some examples without context or email that might look like this. Could you tell me why we've hired a second social media manager for the same client? And here's what this email would look like after you've edited and provided some context. Hi, Alan. I hope you're doing well. I was just reviewing project allocations and had a question. Could you tell me why we've hired a second social media manager for the same client? As you can see, this example starts with a friendly introduction and a sentence to provide some context so the recipient better understands your question when sending an email to someone you don't know. You can't just start with I need your help. You need to introduce yourself first and then provide some context before getting to the main point of your email. Let's look at another before and after example.

Dear Alan, could you please help me get a review in The Washington Post? Here's what the same M.O. would look like after you've edited it and provided some context. Dear Alan, I am Brendin, VP of marketing at ABC Co.. This is your introduction. Jack Collins referred you to me as someone who can help me with public relations here. You're providing context. Could you please help me get a review in The Washington Post? As you can see, Bill, for example, is abrupt and comes off rude. On the other hand, the second example gently introduces the receiver to the objective of the email. It has an introduction and content which will improve the chances of getting a positive response.

In email communication. You need to learn when to respect and ignore hierarchy. Hierarchy is important in business because it separates responsibilities and establishes accountability. But hierarchy also tends to be very stringent because it clearly creates boundaries between people and naturally prevents relationships from evolving. This means that if you want to create a new relationship or improve an existing one, you need to learn when to look past the hierarchy. If you're placed above the other individual, then it is very easy to ignore the hierarchy and even introduce some informal humor in your email.

Now, being more casual in your email sends a message to the subordinate that you're not a stickler for formality. You give them the green light that they need to relax in your presence. And with messages being sent to you, you effectively open the door that will slowly lead to a relationship. The opposite situation is much more difficult. It is more challenging to ignore this hierarchy when you're emailing someone who is more senior than you. So when you're messaging your boss, you cannot ignore the hierarchy and the requirements that you have to abide by unless you already have an informal relationship with them. But when it comes to communication with managers, you're expected to defer to their judgment and show respect. Aside from doing your job well, you can still use email for a building report with your manager. Here are two tricks.

First, you can drop subjects in your email that, you know, appeal to your manager. You can do this by indirectly mentioning his or her interests. For example, if you know your manager is a soccer fan, you can mention something indirect while giving your daily report. For example, Dear Alan, I started a new training program with my team focused on cooperation. My objective is to have them coordinating seamlessly, like Barcelona. So if you're not a football or soccer fan, Barcelona in this case is referring to a professional soccer team in Spain. Similarly, if you know your boss is interested in opera or theater, you can mention something different. Here's an example of what you could say when giving a project appraisal detailing the team's performance was excellent. The way they handled the interchange of tasks was flawless. It was like reading a world class bully. Even the client was thoroughly impressed.

Another way to get your boss out of his shell and improve your relationship with him would be to be really modest. He comes off as humble too, especially when you know that you have an excellent performance at work. More importantly, if your performance is exceptional, your boss would feel compelled to praise you too, which would help to create a closer business relationship. The easiest way to do this would be to praise your team members while letting your input chapter. Besides, your team members will appreciate the extra attention and encouragement. One thing to remember here is this kind of thing only works if your boss is already aware of your excellent performance. In summary, emails can be used to create new relationships as well as improve and maintain existing relationships. The secret to doing this is to find the right balance between formal and informal tone of writing and always providing enough context, as well as knowing when to ignore or respect the hierarchy.

Using Humor in Business Emails

Is it acceptable to use humor in business emails or should you avoid it altogether? Humor in emails can help greatly when it comes to creating relationships or strengthening existing bonds, but it is also capable of ruining them to get the most out of humor emails. You need to know what to do and not to do when using it in this chapter. I'll explain the best ways of using humor in business emails while avoiding the most common pitfalls.

Here's what you're going to learn in this chapter. Why use humor in business emails? The importance of knowing the recipient, avoiding the most dangerous subjects, situational humor and its benefits, and whether it's okay to joke around about people. Relationships are all about personalities because they only form when different personalities work well together. Putting your personality into your email will help you with your business relationships. In other words, a generic tone is safe in business emails, but it's also less effective for forming a new relationship or developing an existing relationship. Further, one way of adding personality to business emails is to introduce humor. But humor in business emails only works if you do it right when inappropriately used humor can easily backfire.

In this chapter, I want to arm you with everything you need to know on how to use humor in your emails and turn a passive, formal and dull business relationship into one that brims with friendship and genuine connection. Now let's take a look at the role humor plays in business emails. Whether you're emailing a subordinate and associate or a superior, breaking through the boundaries established by workplace hierarchy is the first step to forming a relationship or even nudging one to evolve further. The fact that humor works so well at breaking the formal ice is the prime reason why it's so useful when it comes to forming and maintaining relationships. Another reason why humor and email emails can help form and strengthen bonds is that it evokes an emotional response from the reader.

In fact, a joke or even one that's only worthy of a little smile can turn a highly formal announcement focused email into a conversation. On the flip side, humor also has the potential to ruin business relationships. Luckily, the drawbacks of humor only become apparent when it's not used in the right manner. In other words, if you're looking to boost your business relationships by using humor in your emails, you need to do it carefully. The trick to being flawless is to be aware of the dos and don'ts of using humor. It is important to be mindful of how human emotions can go wrong and then working towards avoiding making the same mistakes will now take a look at some of these dos and don'ts. First, knowing the recipient's tastes is important. Knowing the target audience is the single most important aspect of any kind of communication. It is equally important in emails as it is when it comes to public relations and media. If you know your audience well, any kind of message can be tailored to have a maximum impact when it comes to humor in emails.

This means knowing the recipient's preferences. For example, sending a slapstick gift to someone who is very serious and intellectual is not going to have the same effect as a highly intelligent, cerebral joke. Similarly, a joke or anecdote with multiple layers of humor will fall flat if your reader prefers slapstick humor. These aren't the only types of humor either. A couple of other types of humor include wordplay, such as puns and circumstantial humor based on funny situations or scenarios. Matching the recipient's preferences with the right kind of humor is the reason why you need to make sure that you know about the target audience before trying to incorporate humor into your email. Next, you need to be aware of people's sensitivities while knowing what kind of humor the reader likes is possible. You certainly cannot hope to know everything about their life. This is why it is wise to stay on the side of caution when it comes to incorporating humor into your emails. This means avoiding sensitive topics or subjects that can be controversial.

As a result, it is better to avoid talking about things like race, culture, ethnicities, sexual preferences and gender, amongst others. This disqualifies all forms of dark humor as well as dark humor is very subjective and interpretive, which means that it's easy for someone to get offended. You might be wondering, is it OK to joke about situations or people when trying to incorporate humor into your emails? It is best to focus on situations as opposed to individuals. When you focus on situations and circumstances, you take away all possibilities of individuals or communities being involved.

Naturally, this reduces the chances of anyone getting offended. One way you can joke about people in your email is if you joke about yourself. So self-deprecating humor works because nobody can get offended about you making fun of yourself. It's safe, reliable, and you're more entitled to make fun of yourself than anyone else on the planet. In summary, when you incorporate humor into your email, you can get an emotional reaction from the reader, which in turn helps form bonds and improve relationships. But to do this properly, you need to know your audience, avoid sensitive subjects, and appropriately use humor about situations and people.

Building Credibility In Business Emails

To form a lasting and fruitful business relationship, you need to build your credibility with your business contacts because credibility implies trust and belief between professionals while building credibility using business models is not an easy task. It is very much possible to have the right knowledge. And that's exactly what we're going to cover in this chapter and this chapter. You're going to learn what is credibility in business, why it is important how to protect the recipient's identity, the importance of honoring commitments, using attachments to build credibility and disclaimers, e-mail privacy policies and your credibility.

Credibility is a fundamental part of any relationship. If someone doesn't believe or trust you, then it is very difficult for that individual to work with you. The only problem is that building credibility is much more difficult at a distance than it is face to face. It's not that difficult to imagine why either. When you're not face to face, you don't have the benefit of facial expressions and bodily gestures to enforce or underline the words being said. In fact, building credibility is especially challenging through text based communication channels such as emails, because along with facial expressions and your gestures, you also lose the benefit of vocal variations and tones. But this doesn't mean that it's not possible. It is very much possible, provided you know what credibility means and what you need to do to build it.

In this chapter, I will not only define credibility, but also explain what you need to do and how to build it through business emails to get started. I'd like to address the question, what is credibility in business when it comes to building credibility using emails? Your objective is to get the recipient to trust you, to see what you mean and do what you say. In other words, credibility and business is all about authenticity. And this can be built through repeatedly honoring promises, regardless of whether they are subtle or openly made. Since the medium of communication is emails, your email becomes your representative.

How it looks, sounds and what it contains become the aspects that affect your credibility. So if you can manage and manipulate these aspects in your email, you can slowly build credibility in the eyes of the recipient. Let's see how you can go about doing this. First, protect their identity. Email addresses are like real home addresses. People don't want them to be advertised freely. They want them kept private, especially in today's world of nonstop spam inboxes.

As a result, the absolute minimum a professional expects from a business contact is that their email address is kept safe. So if the professional finds out that the email was shared further without their consent, it will automatically result in a loss of credibility for the person who did the sharing. This is why the first thing they need to do to build credibility via business emails is to make sure that you protect your business's contacts and email addresses. This is easy to do. This can be achieved by getting their consent before sharing their email address. Another important thing you need to do is to honor commitments and promises. Credibility is the belief that what is being said is true and what is being promised will be honored. So if you're trying to build your credibility via business emails, you need to make sure that all the information shared in your email is true and accurate.

This means checking the emails content before pressing the send button and not ignoring the proofreading and editing responsibilities. Similarly, if you want to be considered a credible professional, you need to make sure that you honor your commitments. This means being very deliberate about your commitments and not making promises that you cannot keep. A good example of this would be giving a deadline of three to four days away. Even if you think the current project will only take two days to complete, the extra day or two will give you margin for error. And even if you deliver the project early, it will help your credibility. You'll also have to make sure to meet your obligations. If you've agreed to a deadline and you're falling behind, then you may want to put in that extra time to meet that deadline to retain your credibility.

If you know that you're missing a promised deadline, it's always better to let the concerned party know well in advance. They will find out sooner or later by telling them sooner you're at least establishing honesty, which will help you credibility. This brings me to the next important tip you need to protect attachments or links with passwords. Your credibility will always be helped by the recipient's perception of how well you take care of information. This is especially relevant when it comes to sensitive or confidential information. There are two things you need to do to show that you treat confidential and sensitive information responsibly. The first thing is to never include this kind of information in the main content or body of the email.

As this information could be accessed by Internet service providers and the tech team of the business, the alternative is to send this information and attach files or links to files that have been uploaded on third party websites such as Dropbox or Google Drive. And the second thing you need to do is to always encrypt or password protect these files. Almost all software programs, including Adobe Acrobat or Microsoft Office, come with an encryption feature that prevents the file from being opened without a password. If a software doesn't have this facility, then the file can be compressed into a zip file, for example, or something with a layer of password protection. Next, let's take a look at how you can include disclaimer or privacy statements, apart from actually protecting the information you're sharing in your email through encryptions and passwords.

You can also give it legal protection by including disclaimers or privacy statements at the end of your email. The purpose of email disclaimers is to inform the recipients that information being shared in the email is confidential and cannot be reproduced or shared without the consent of the people involved. Email disclaimers can help build credibility because they show that you're a professional and that you're aware of legal liabilities and that you know how to protect information and know the value of personal information.

In summary, building credibility using business emails is all about creating the right impression and making the recipients trust your professionalism and authenticity. You can build your credibility by protecting the recipient's identity, honoring commitments professionally, protecting, providing information, using passwords and using disclaimers or email privacy policies. I'll see you in the next chapter.

Modifying Emails to Cope with Cultural Nuances

When trying to build a relationship or strengthen an existing one through business emails, cultural nuances can get in the way of causing miscommunication and resentment. The only way to prevent this from happening is to be aware of this possibility and modify emails to reflect the relevant cultural differences. This chapter aims to help professionals identify cultural nuances that may affect their business relationship and prevent misunderstandings by changing their emails. Here's what we're going to cover: how cultural nuances affect business, email communications, changing radio style to reflect global English norms, conforming to internationally accepted formatting standards.

And lastly, be mindful of cultural differences and cope with them appropriately. Cultural differences play a major role in how people communicate when the cultural differences are big. You have to work harder to create and maintain your business relationships. But this doesn't mean that people from similar cultures with comparable values don't have cultural differences to cope with. In fact, they do. Which is why it's so important for all professionals to learn how to modify their language based on the global English mindset and change their writing style in a way that their emails make sense despite various cultural differences.

After this chapter, you will have all the skills and knowledge required to write such emails. To write effective emails, you need to change your writing to conform to global English norms. The most important thing you need to do to modify your email to cope with cultural differences is to do culture. Is it? In other words, you need to write in a way that doesn't contain religion or culture specific references. This means neutralizing all verbs, phrases, idioms, slang and references that you would normally use in your day to day life. In place of these, you'll need to make sure that your language is purposeful to the point so it comes off as neutral and practical. Here are some examples of words with different meanings between two cultures, the US and the UK.

First, the word coach refers to a sports teacher in the US, but to Abbas in the UK, no to trainer. This means someone who trains in the United States but a sports shoe in the UK. Number three, lift and elevator in the UK is what you use to go up floors in a building while the Americans use the word elevator. Another important tip is to adhere to global formatting standards. While language specific differences are more diverse across cultures, there are formatting based differences. A good example of this is format's. Here is how the meaning of 12, 10, 20, 20 changes from the US to other parts of the world. In the US, it stands for December 10th, 2020 and in some other parts of the world, October 12th, 2020.

The difference is huge and that can result in considerable misunderstandings. This is why it needs to be taken into account when you're writing dates and your email. Formatting is also a concern when writing time since the recipient of your email may be in a different time zone. The global business standard is to either use the Greenwich Mean Time GMT or the universal coordinated time U.S. team when scheduling meetings or discussing deadlines. When it comes to time, you'll always have to pay attention to how cultures affect working hours. Here are two examples of how this happens. The first example is France. The French citizens have the right to disconnect, which allows them to completely disconnect from work beyond working hours. It's a cultural trade that's enforced through law.

As a result, many French professionals don't entertain business contacts after 6pm and on their days off. To give you another example, in some Islamic nations, Fridays are considered to be a holy day. As a result, in some nations, Fridays and Saturdays are considered to be the weekend, while Sunday is seen as a working day. Next, you need to pay attention to cultural differences. What is seen as proper business communication etiquette also varies from one nation to another. In fact, the variation is so diverse and widespread that it can be difficult to qualify it in one category. The closest anyone has ever come to understanding and describing and categorizing cultural differences in business communication is Edward Hull in nineteen seventy four whole categories of cultures into two categories, which were low context cultures and high context cultures.

How differentiated between cultures on the basis of how direct and to the point. The professionals expected business communication to be so professional and low context. Cultures tend to be very concise and direct in their business communication, which means that they don't exchange pleasantries and they just get straight to business professionals from high context. Cultures, on the other hand, expect pleasantries and business communication and if the emails are direct when they might find it rude or offensive. High context cultures also value harmony and well-being of the group versus individual needs and focus on building personal relationships and business communication.

Here are a couple of examples how emails from low context cultures can differ from high context cultures. Let's look at an example from a low context culture. Hi David, how are you? I wanted to inquire about the deadline for the next shipment as we're trying to streamline allocations here. Could you let me know when the supplies will be dispatched? Thanks in regards, Dennis. Here's how email could be used in high context culture. Hi, David. How are you? I read about the heat wave in your city. I hope the family and kids are all doing fine, especially with the holiday season coming up. Please convey my wishes.

I'm emailing because I wanted to confirm the deadline for the next shipment as we're trying to streamline allocations here. Could you let me know when the supplies will be dispatched as that would help me delegate tasks and boost production here? Thanks. In regards, Dennis, some examples of low context cultures are the US, UK, Germany or India, China, Japan, Spain and the Middle East can be seen as high context cultures. Identifying which type of cultures or recipients belong to is important because it will allow you to tailor your employer to suit their expectations. In summary, cultural differences between two professionals can significantly affect their business relationship. This is why it is the responsibility of every professional to modify their email to reflect the cultural nuances they're dealing with. This means conforming to global English norms, sticking to internationally accepted formatting standards and paying attention to cultural differences that are unique in every situation.

Email Communication Across the Generational Gap

People from different generations can differ in various ways, including perspectives, perceptions and personalities. These differences are so entrenched that building relationships with emails between generations might be a challenge, but it is very much possible with some awareness and precautions in this chapter. You learn about the impact of generational gaps in business email communication and how the resulting problems can be prevented.

Here's a quick overview of what topics we're going to cover the changing workforce, landscape and generational diversity, email, communication and generational challenges various ways through which the generational gaps can be bridged, how using multiple media can help, why keeping a generic tone is important and the importance of asking and giving clarification. Generational separation is as important in business email communication as cultural and geographical separation. This is especially true in the modern workplace, which has changed drastically in the last few years. According to the US Bureau of Labor Statistics, the number of employed people older than 55 years old has risen in recent years. This isn't just an American trend, though. As the global population becomes older, the average employee age is going up all over the world.

At the same time, the younger generation is starting to join the workforce. You need to keep in mind that individuals and each generation have had political, social, economic and technological experiences that are completely unique to them. The direct result is that people from these different generations communicate differently. Naturally, this affects email communication. The limitations of text based communication channels, such as emails, amplify the interpersonal difficulties, miscommunications and conflicts that may be caused by these generational differences. But there are ways through which these generational differences can be bridged in email communication. In this chapter, you will learn about these ways and how to implement them. Text is subjective. Even without generational differences, sentences can be interpreted in multiple ways.

This is particularly true in English. Here are a few examples of sentences that are structurally simple. But each of them has two different meanings, depending on your perspective. For example, the old man hit the boy with an umbrella. Was the boy holding the umbrella or was he hit by one? The man gave his dog food. Was he fed dog food or was his dog fed food? Let's look at another example. Press the button on the right now. Is the button located on the right side or are you supposed to press the right side of the button? Check the drop down menu in the middle? Is the drop down menu in the middle or are you supposed to check its middle options?

Fill the form at the bottom? Is the form at the bottom or do you need to fill the bottom part of the form? Do you see how even simple sentences can be pretty confusing and result in different applications? When very generational differences come into play and the sentence has become more complex, it can result in a lot of misinterpretations. The simple solution to this problem is to use more than just text to convey your message in business. Email communication visuals can be instrumental in avoiding miscommunication and resulting conflicts. This is particularly true for screenshots, gifts and even chapters showing elaborate procedures. Adding visuals to your email will support your message and help the receiver understand what you're trying to say. If you're not close with the recipient, it's best to keep your tone neutral.

Avoid using jokes, sarcasm, emojis and gifs as these can be counterproductive. When you're working with someone you don't really know well, some people might view them as too casual and inappropriate for business communication. Another great example of how personality in emails can cause problems between generations are ellipses. Older generations use ellipses as a way to show that they've run out of things to say in a very neutral and nonjudgmental manner. For example, this sounds like a great idea with an ellipse at the end. In contrast, younger generations that have grown up with clearer character restrictions use ellipses as a message. For example, ellipsis can be interpreted as a passive aggressive message by some millennials. The same sentence that sounds like a great idea with an ellipse at the end could actually mean that the sender is being sarcastic and is not generally supportive of that idea.

It's very subtle that punctuation can have a big impact on your relationships with your colleagues. So you need to be aware of how you use it and when communicating across various generations. Such differences are even backed up by a few surveys. Here's an interesting study conducted by Granularly.

Grumbly found that employees under the age of 35 were 50 percent more likely to be told that they are too informal by older generations. This might mean that the younger generation is less formal in email communication. Another similar finding was that 88 percent of the people below 35 years of age thought that using exclamation marks on an animal was OK, while only 30 percent of people above 65 years old agreed.

Do you see how punctuation plays an important part in your daily life? Education, whether it's ellipses, exclamation marks or other writing behavior, is better to follow generic email practices and remove these kinds of generation specific traits from your email message that will help you minimize miscommunication between generations. Even if you take precautions, such as using multiple media within an email and keeping things as generic as possible, it is still possible for generational gaps to cause miscommunication. Generational differences are essentially gaps in perspectives, perceptions and personalities, which cannot be bridged flawlessly through words alone. This is why it's better to be aware that they can come up and be prepared in advance.

The simplest way of dealing with miscommunication caused by generational gaps is to be open about seeking and giving clarification. These types of miscommunications are usually very subtle, as was obvious with ellipses, exclamation marks and graphics. A simple clarification can fix the problem and help you maintain healthy relationships with your colleagues. Generational diversity in the workplace has gradually increased in the last few years. In emails, the limitations of textual communication can get augmented by generational gaps. The best way to deal with these types of miscommunication is to use multiple media within emails, keep the tone generic and be open to seeking and giving clarification.

Section Three

All Ima's, no matter how formal or informal, have a basic structure to improve your email writing skills, you need to start with these fundamental elements. The subject line greetings, the main body, the supporting information and the sign-off. This chapter includes chapters on each of the five core email segments. In this overview, you'll find a brief on each of the chapters. You can also come back to the chapter to revise everything you learned in the upcoming chapters and email is simply the evolved form of the traditional letter similar to traditional letter.

What an email can be divided into separate segments, even though your relationship with a receiver will always take priority. Each of the five core elements of email is important when it comes to writing the email. The reason for this is that every one of these core elements has its unique purpose in the structure. As a result, how you approach each segment needs to take into account this purpose. For this reason, study each of the five core elements individually, and the first chapter will focus on how to write effective subject lines. The purpose of the subject line is to tell the recipients why the email was sent to them.

From this perspective, it performs the same function that the headline performs for a new space. It not only informs the recipients about the purpose of the email, but also delivers other associate information, such as whether the email is urgent or if it includes an attachment. In the chapter on subject lines, you'll learn more about how subject lines affect the recipient's mindset and how they're related to the information inside the email. Apart from this, the chapter will also delve into how long a subject line can be and what can be done to make it sound more urgent. In the second chapter, we'll cover writing email greetings. It is a mistake to take email greetings lightly. They have their unique purpose in the email infrastructure and are only secondary to the subject lines and importance.

They not only have an emotional impact on the recipients in the beginning of the email, but also on the sender in subtle ways. Email greetings are technically important too, because they're shown a snippet and the recipient's inbox in the chapter on email greetings. I'll be elaborating further on their importance and how you can manipulate them to ensure a positive impact on the recipient. A big part of the chapter will focus on specific types of email greetings and scenarios in which they're most effective, next. And chapter three will focus on the body of the email and discuss what to keep in mind while writing the main content.

The main content of an email is where the most important information is conveyed by the sender to the receiver. This, along with the fact that the main body is often the largest, makes it the most vital component of the email. Its immense importance means that the main content needs to be structured in the most coherent and rational way possible. If the main content does not flow logically, the reader may quit without reading the whole email. This is why in the chapter on the main content, I talk about how to structure it using a technique that journalists use all over the world. Along with this, I'll explain what the sender can do to ensure that their message is understood and that the recipient responds quickly and appropriately. And chapter five will cover how to provide supporting information in your email. Supporting information is usually included in complex and long emails.

The purpose of supporting information is to make the content easier to understand. But it's also important because it prevents the email from getting too long and convoluted. In this chapter covering supporting information, I'll explain how we can either improve the understanding of the reader or confuse the issue. Apart from this, I'll describe the three different ways that supporting information can be provided in the email. In chapters six you learn about using the right sign offs and signatures of and signatures can be used to enter the email. As a result, they leave a lasting impression on the recipient.

This is why sign offs and signatures need to be consistent with other elements of the email. This means that sign offs and signatures need to match the primary object of the email, the overall context and the underlying relationship between the sender and the receiver in the chapter covering this element. I first explained what sign offs and signatures are. Then I focus on the various ways the sign offs can be used before describing the various components of the signatures and how they can be formatted. Are you ready to dive in? I'll see you in the next chapter.

How to Write Effective Subject Lines

The subject line is one of the most important elements of every email that you send. This means two things. First, it cannot be misleading in any way, even by mistake. And second, it needs to be true to the main purpose behind the email. While you get better at writing your subject lines with some practice, it will happen if you don't know the fundamentals in this chapter, we're going to discuss those fundamentals. In this chapter, we're going to cover the following topics. Why subject lines are important and how they affect the reader, the relationship between the subject lines and emails, the proper length and format of each subject line, how to make subject lines more urgent and ensure a quick response. Here's a fun fact.

Did you know that forty seven out of every 100 people open their emails based on the subject line? Does that surprise you? It shouldn't, because the subject line is an email. What a headline is to a news article. And most of us only read the newspapers based on whether the headline appeals to us or not. The same study also found that 64 percent of individuals open emails based on the sender. If they recognize the sending address, they open the email and if not, they don't. So other than the relationship between the sender and the receiver of the email, the single most important aspect of an email is the subject line.

This is why in this chapter, we will explore the importance of subject lines while learning the best techniques for making them effective. First, let's take a look at the relationship between subject lines and emails. In practical terms, you can view the subject line as the title or heading of your email. It defines the email as a message. It tells the reader whether the email is worth opening, how urgent it is, and, most importantly, its overall purpose. This is why when writing the subject line, you need to make sure that it conveys the primary purpose of the e-mail message. Let's look at some examples of various situations and what subject lines would be appropriate.

First, if someone referred, you make sure you write referred by X, Y, Z. If you're following up on a previous email mention, follow up on three. If you're inviting someone, write an invitation for ABC, meeting four. If you're making a request, I appeal by saying request for and explain the reason. Five. Finally, if you're talking about a specific project or order mentioning the project name or the order ID at the beginning, such as order number one, two, three, four, five, or even regarding Project A.B.C., now you might be wondering how long your subject line should be? The next thing you need to keep in mind while writing the subject line is its length. You can't have a subject line that goes rambling on forever and ever.

You need to keep it short and crisp, preferably less than forty characters. The forty character limit is imposed by most email platforms, while some even chapter the subject line as short as thirty characters. So what does this mean? It means that the subject line the reader sees in his inbox is shortened to fit into the available space. Here's an example. If you write a subject line that says We would like to invite you to our annual celebration to be held at the Albert Hall, the reader will get a subject line that shows a chapterped version like this. Well, it may create suspense in the mind of some readers, it doesn't convey much beyond the fact that the email is an invitation and ambiguity is something you need to avoid business communication at all costs. So you would be better off writing the short subject line.

For example, ABC's annual celebration invitation. This way the reader will see the full text and know he is being invited to the annual celebration of the company ABC. And just because they recommend shorter subject lines, this doesn't mean that the other extreme of the spectrum is acceptable. In other words, you can't ever leave the subject line blank. Not only will this irritate the receiver who may or may not delete it, you'll also be risking a shortcut to the spam folder. Next, let's discuss formatting the subject line. The subject lines don't need any embellishments, especially in business communication. Here's a quick tip that will help you when you're writing your subject line, and that's following the U.S. Navy's KISS principle. ISIS is an acronym for Keepit Stupid, Simple or Keep It Simple, Stupid.

The principle is basically the U.S. Navy version of minimalism. The U.S. Navy would follow this principle whatever they were devising a new system or strategy. Naturally, this technique applies to subject lines to what does this mean in practice, however, it means avoiding a series of punctuation marks like this, emojis and sentences using all caps. This might look like you're shouting again. Don't take this minimalism too far.

Don't remove punctuation marks altogether you don't want. Let's eat grammar when you want to just say let's eat grandma.

As shown in this example, adding a simple comma can completely change the meaning of the sentence. Now, moving on, let's see how you can create a sentence of urgency with subject lines. What if your email is very important and you want a quick response? There are ways of doing this while keeping the KISS principle in mind. The first is to use the high priority feature available. Most email platforms using this feature will result in there being an urgent icon, typically a star or a red exclamation mark before your subject line in the reader's inbox.

Another method is to start your subject line with the word urgent, important, or even need a response. You can even make it all caps if you want, provided that is just a word or two and not long sentences. The third and the best method is to construct your subject line in a way that the most important information comes first. For example, instead of writing information regarding your complaint for invoice number one, one, two, two, three, three refunds, you should write a refund process for invoice number and stay the number.

Usually the last method should be enough for most email messages. The other methods should only be used in more urgent situations. The bottom line is that your subject line should tell the reader what to expect inside the email. It should neither oversell or undersell the purpose of the email and should be brief and straightforward.

Why Should You Focus On Your Greetings

Imar Greetings seems simple and routine, but that's not always the case. They affect how the receivers perceive you, whether they open the email or not, and even how they respond to it. In fact, next to the subject lines, the email's greetings are their most important elements. This is why it's so important that you pay special attention to your email greetings instead of taking them lightly as to how you should direct their special focus.

The answer is in this chapter. In this chapter, we're going to learn how email greetings affect the recipient's mindset and response to the email message, which can be used while writing email greetings. How to use the recipient's name and email greetings. And should context affect Ebong Greening's? There are three reasons why email greetings are important to have an external impact and one has an internal effect. Let me explain what I mean by this. Most of you already know the first of the three reasons as the first impression is psychology.

The first impression is known as the anchoring bias. By definition, anchoring bias is a cognitive bias. Where an individual depends too heavily on an initial piece of information is a hidden preconception that's inherent deep within our psyche that makes us lose our objectivity. Can you see how this could apply to email? Greetings. Your email greetings are the first thing the receiver will see after the subject line, and these will affect their objectivity in one way or another. That's just human nature. While the subject line will tell the reader what your email is about, your greetings will be at the top of the email, setting the tone. If the greetings are not right, the readers will automatically get put off.

The second reason, while greetings are important, is not as scientific as the first one, but it's definitely technical in nature. If you look at your inbox, you'll see that each email shows up in the following format, the name of the sender subject line and a short snippet. As you can see, the short snippet has the first few lines of your email, including the greetings. Even before the readers open your email, they have already been affected by your greetings. Just like in human interactions, first impressions in email communication have a long lasting effect. The third and final reason why email greetings are important is internal. This means that it affects you rather than the reader.

Most people write their email greetings before the body of the email message. As a result, what they write in the greetings affects how they approach the body of the email. For example, if you open with to whom it may concern, you immediately detach from the email and make it formal. But if you write Hi David, your matter will be warmer and more casual. Next, let's look at ways you can personalize your greetings to connect with the recipient. First, you'll need to start with the reader's name. It is natural for people to respond positively to their names. You can use this to your advantage by including the recipient's name and your email and email greeting that includes the recipient's name will be much better and more personable than one that doesn't, if you don't know the recipient's name, make an effort to find it by checking the business team's page, LinkedIn, or even calling the company and asking up front.

Imagine reaching out to a new contact. You can either start with Dear Sir or Dear John. The second option will yield a much more positive response than the first one. It will help you connect with the recipient and show that you put in some effort to look up their name. Next, let's take a look at the tone and email greetings. There are two types of tone you can really take with the business email, and it depends solely on your relationship with the recipient. If you don't know the reader at all, your email greeting needs to be formal and if you're on good terms with them, your greetings can be semi-formal. Let me show you how each one works.

First is the formal tone. If you're not close to the receiver, it's best to begin with, dear, followed by their title and the name of the individual. So if you're sending the email to John Smith, Ukrainians can be like this. Dear Mr. Smith, using the person's last name. Dear Mr. John, sometimes people use the receiver's first name. Dear Dr. Smith, if he's a physician or has a doctorate, if the recipient is a woman, the doctor stays the same. But the mister needs to be changed to miss. It shouldn't be Mrs. since there's too much ambiguity about a person's marital status. Unless, Of course, you know what their marital status is, so it becomes. Dear Miss Jane, dear Miss Smith, dear Dr. Smith. Or if you're implying more than one person and you're upfront about it, you can approach the scenario in two different ways.

No, if you're implying more than one person and are upfront about it, you can approach the scenario in two different ways. First, if there are only two to four people, you can write their names with commas such as Dear John, Jane and Justin. If you're sending the email to a lot of people, you can simply change the greeting to say, dear all or to your team. Next, you have a semi formal tone. If you've known the reader for some time and have a less formal relationship with them, you can replace dear with hi or hello and drop the title completely. You can combine this with the first name. Your greetings will end up looking like this. Hi John or hello John. If you're sending it to a group of people, your email greeting will look like this. Hi, John. Jane and Justin or hi all or even. Hi, everybody.

Next on the list are email greetings for follow ups and replies, the examples we've already talked about. Abode will be suitable for virtually every email message you'll ever send, they're safe, fairly neutral and as repeatable as you want them to be. But what if there has been a lack of back and forth on the emails in such scenarios? You can do away with standard email greetings and make your openings more contextual. Let's have a look at them first if your last discussion was on the phone. You can start with us for our phone discussion or even as discussed on the phone, too. If you're responding to a previously made commitment or request, you could write as requested, as promised. Here's more information on three.

If you're doing the traditional follow up, you can go with just following up on, just wanting to make sure of that thought. I'll check it out. Can you please update me on four? And if you're only acknowledging a previous email you can open with.

Thank you for getting back to me. Thanks for your prompt response and thanks for the update. In a nutshell, your email greetings are important because they influence the recipients first impression. Show up as a snippet in the inbox and set the tone for the rest of the email for you while writing the email greetings. You can expect a better response if you use the recipient's names, use the right tone for your relationship, or make the greetings more contextual. I'll see you in the next chapter.

Writing the Main Content

The main body of your email will provide the most important information for the receiver, this information needs to only be provided in the most logical way possible, but also in a way that makes it easy to understand. If the main body of your email is incoherent and confusing, then this can either result in your email getting ignored or leading to a lot of back and forth for clarification. This chapter will teach you how to keep that from happening.

Here's a quick overview of what we're going to cover. Writing the opening sequence with an inverted pyramid technique working backward from the opening sentences to give more information about the primary purpose of the email, finishing off by sharing what the receiver is expected to do. The subject lines and greetings will always be important because they set the stage for your email. But once they've done the job of getting the recipient interested, the actual information will be provided by the body of the email. In simple words, the subject line and the greetings are accessories for the centerpiece that is the body of the email. So the purpose of the body of the email is to present the relevant information most logically and sensibly to the recipient.

And when a response is required, the purpose of the body of the email is to persuade the recipient to give that response. So you've taken some writing Books in the past. You might have heard of the technique called inverted pyramid technique. Journalists use a technique called inverted pyramid in their work. This technique requires you to put the most important information first and then mention things in decreasing order of importance you're approached with. The opening sequence needs to be the same. The trick here is to share the main message first in one or two sentences. Let's take a closer look at some examples.

One, if you're introducing yourself, you can write my name is Jessica and I would like to introduce myself as your account manager at ABC. Insert your company name here, too. If your email is about a specific project, you can see this is in reference to the upcoming email campaign. Three, If it's an invitation email, you can write. We would like to invite you to our annual conference and tradeshow to be held on September 30th. As you can see in all of these examples, the email started off with the most important details to catch the reader's attention and provide them with enough context to keep reading.

Now let's take a look at how you can answer questions and elaborate. Once you've established the baseline with the opening sequence, it's time to provide more information to support it. The best way to do this is to start with a baseline and then work backward with your reasoning, justifications and flow of thought. The sentences or even paragraphs that follow through will change based on the purpose of the email. These paragraphs are important because they will prevent needless back and forth for clarification and explanations. To make this work, you need to get into the head of the reader and preempt any questions they may have about the opening sequence. Let's see some examples.

One, since it's unlikely that you would introduce yourself to someone without an objective, you could show your objective after the first sentence. An account manager, for example, can explain what services he can provide to the receiver, too. If you're asking for the project deadlines to be extended, you can explain why you feel this is required and share more details about the delays or problems that the project has been facing. Three In the case of an invitation, you can explain where the event will be held, what is expected from the receiver, how they should confirm their participation and what would be expected from them if they decide to participate. If the event repeats regularly, its history can be shared as well.

While it's important to provide as much information as possible on the body of the email, you shouldn't go overboard with it either. It's very easy to follow the flow of information in your head and put all of it down in the body of the email. But you need to sort through all the information and only share the bits that are relevant to the receiver. Here's some examples of how people could share too much information and common mistakes that they can make. One in an introduction email. If you go into too much detail describing your career path and talking about yourself, then you might be wasting the receiver's time, too. If you start sharing how difficult your project team is to work with, you're not only giving irrelevant information but also being a professional.

An example. Three, if you start sharing how many invitations have been sent or how the event is being organized, you're giving information that might be useless to the reader. The next thing you should do is clearly state what you expect from the reader. At the end of the body of the email, you have to clearly state what you expect from the receiver to prevent any confusion. This does two things. First, it reaffirms the purpose of your email. And second, it subliminally encourages the receiver to do what you want them to do. It's also important that the final part of your email body is polite and positive to create the right lasting impression.

Let's see some examples when introducing yourself. You can finish the email by saying, please feel free to get in touch with me in any of the following ways. If you want the project deadlines to be extended, you can say, please let me know as soon as the decision is made on the extension. If you're inviting a guest, an event you can write, hoping for a positive confirmation from your end.

To summarize, the email body can be divided into three segments. The first sentence provides the most important information to the recipient, and the second segment supports the first couple of sentences and addresses any potential questions the receiver may have while the final segment tells the receiver what the sender's expectations are. I'll see you in the next chapter.

Providing Supporting Information

When you need to send complex messages and emails, you need to back up your primary message with supporting information, it's vital that the supporting information is provided in the right way. So you don't confuse the recipient. The three main ways of providing supporting information are within the email text as attachments and through annotated screenshots. This chapter will teach you how to provide supporting information in your emails so the recipient can easily understand your message. Here's what we're going to cover.

Using fax documents and other resources are supporting information using simple supporting information in the email text, multiple things to consider when appending attachments and adding screenshots to share complex instructions. While many business emails are basic updates on ongoing projects or discussions, some can be quite involved in elaborate. Sometimes entire conversations can take place in search email threads. Some of these emails represent the earlier stages of a long running negotiation between the representatives of two different companies. And then there are those marathon business emails that I send to teams as instruction manuals or those that double up as proposals to potential clients, irrespective of their underlying purpose.

These long business emails almost always carry huge amounts of information. They have the standard opening and closing sequences, but in the middle there is a large chunk of supporting information. Usually the supporting information is factual in nature, depending on how the supporting information is provided and presented, it can either make the message confusing or make it clear for the receiver. The supporting information can also end up annoying the receiver if you're not careful, which will not help your primary objective.

Fortunately, you can ensure that the supporting information helps your cause rather than working against it by choosing to present it in the right medium. There are basically three ways through which you can provide supporting information in a business. Email will analyze each one of them individually in this chapter. One way is in text form. The simplest and easiest way to support information to email is to do it within the body of the main content. The only problem is that you can't allow the main body to become too long because most people tend to shy away from long texts.

Keep in mind that people have a busy schedule and a lot of emails and inboxes so they may not have enough time to read through really long emails. This means you can't include too much supporting information in the main content of your email. Besides, it's not like you can cut and paste a 30 page contract proposal in the main body. The obvious question then is what kind of support information can you include in the main body of your email?

My suggestion would be to use simple supportive information like names, numbers, dates, times and even some short updates can be included in the main body. Here are a few examples.

You can include time and location related details. It will look a little bit like this meeting organizer Victoria Miah participants. Valerie Smith, John Edwards, Chris Michael Time 12:00 p.m., October 5th, 2020. Location Conference Room three company headquarters agenda quarterly goal setting. Now, let's look at another example. If you're processing and complaining that requires technical support, you can include the following related details. Here's what kind of support information you should add.

Complaint reference, no complaint. Details such as malfunctioning printer. Take a timeline, for example, opened January 5th. Twenty twenty departments respond, for example, in progress resolution time, seven days. As you can see in the examples I showed you, the supporting information in the email text needs to be simple and straightforward when adding supporting information. Think about why you're writing the message and only include details that are relevant and important to the receiver. Another way to provide information is in an attached file. It's one of the most commonly used methods in email.

Communication attachments are a safe way to provide support information for your email, but you need to be careful about certain things. The first of these things is that if you're attaching a file in your email, you need to mention it in your email body. If you don't mention it in the body of the email, then it can be missed by the receiver and even mistaken as a virus. You can say something simple like this. Please see the document attached in the resources chapter of the Book. I'll share lots of other examples on how to let the recipient know about the attachment. The majority of technologically aware business people don't open attachments unless they're completely sure of the source. So the recipients don't know you personally. They might be hesitant to open your attachment.

Apart from mentioning the attachment in the body of the email, it's also critical that you review your attachment before attaching it in your review. Make sure to look at the following four things. The first one is the filename file names need to reflect the content of the attachment. Never touch a file with a name like Untitled New or document one. Always rename it to reflect the purpose of the file. For example, a training manual. Also, if you've been modifying, exchanging the same file back and forth, make sure to update versions by putting numbers at the end of the file name such as the one B two and three. Or you can see the file name one, two and three. The second thing to look at is format.

The attachments need to be in easily recognizable form. A good example of this is Adobe Photoshop. Graphic designers working in the software work on extensions like Paudie, but a lot of. Clients don't have access to the software and therefore won't be able to open these types of files. So in this case, this is not a suitable format to send clients unless they specifically requested it. This is why designers convert their files to other common image formats before sending them in an email. Now, the third thing to pay attention to is file size. Avoid sending very large files in terms of size. Larger attachments can take a very long time to download and will almost always annoy the recipient.

Besides, most email platforms have size limits that will prevent your huge attachment from even showing up in the inbox. So it's always best to compress the file in a commonly used format. If you're sending photos or documents, put them in a single file first, or you can also save the files with a third party service provider such as Google Drive or Dropbox and share the appropriate link. Another common way to share supporting information is to use screenshots. Screenshots can be both static and animated. Static screenshots are photographs of your screen, while animated screenshots are gifts that can be used to share quick instructions. Screenshots, whether it's static or animated with well-placed annotations can make a huge difference when it comes to explaining a process or a system.

Also, screenshots are great for sharing step by step digital procedures or instructions. This makes screenshots excellent for team communication, a good example of how they can be used as well discussing design samples. There are various browser extensions, standalone software and online screenshot services that can be used to create and edit your screenshots. Using these kinds of tools, you can circle relevant areas, number them, or even put notes right beside the screenshots. There are two ways through which screenshots can be used as supporting information.

The first is to share them as attachments. The second is to paste them within the body of the email. The second option should only be used if the screenshot is small in size. To sum up the whole picture, the supporting information in your email is important because it supports your email with facts, illustrations and other resources. You can provide it in three different ways inside the body as an attachment or within screenshots. I'll see you in the next chapter.

Using the Right Sign-offs And Signatures

Like all other elements of a good email, the sign off his signature has specific purposes. This is why it's so important to ensure that they're consistent with the main purpose of the email. The overall context of the message and your specific relationship with the reader, if they're inconsistent or even missing your email, would not only be misunderstood, but can also end up looking odd to the recipient. You can use this chapter on the intricacies of sign ups and signatures to stop this from happening to you. Here's what we're going to learn. Understanding what spin offs are the most commonly used types of sign offs, understanding what signatures are, various components of email signatures and formatting the signatures in the right way.

It is important to end the email in the same way that you started it with professionalism and accuracy. When the tone of a document changes in the middle, it can be very jarring for the reader. This is why, if you deviate from the established tone and style in the final element of your email, you risk leaving a bad impression on the recipient. The final element of a good email consists of two things. These are the sign offs and the signatures. But before we jump in, what is a sign of exactly? The Merriam Webster Dictionary defines the verb to sign off as to announce the end of something.

So the purpose of a signing off in your email is to literally announce the end of your email. How you sign off in your email should ideally reflect your relationship with the recipient as well as the context of the email. Broadly speaking, there are three types of sign offs that can be used. Let's look at each one of them one by one. First, you have formal sign offs. Formal sign ups are the most commonly used in business communication. They are all weather sign offs that can be used at the end of all emails, regardless of the context. But they're most appropriate if you have a formal relationship with the recipient.

Here are some examples of formal sign offs. Regards, kind regards, warm regards, best regards sincerely. Then you have grateful sign ups. Grateful sign offs can be used in two ways. The first is generic, whereby by using the sign off, you're simply showing that you're grateful for the recipient for reading your email. The second is more specific where you're grateful because of something urgent the recipient did for you. The following are the most commonly used, grateful sign offs. Thank you. Thank you.

Things, many things respectfully and gratefully, and the third hour long form sign offs. You can turn any sentence into a long form sign off, which means that these types of sign offs can be used in various scenarios. Usually, though, they're used as gentle reminders to the receiver that responding to the email is necessary. At the same time, they can be used if you want to sign up to be a little less formal and a little more emotional. Here are three examples of long form sign offs. Looking forward to hoping for a quick response. Let me know what you think. The first one has an emotional component to it, while the last to softly nudge the recipient toward a particular action and the Book resources. I've provided you with many options for sign offs you can use while writing your emails. You can browse through these and pick one that's most appropriate in your situation.

Next, I'd like to discuss email signatures. The signoff should always be followed by a good signature. The simple purpose of the signature is to let the recipient know who sent the email in business communication though WHO is more than just the name. This is why your signature needs to be the recipient of even more information. So where relevant, you must try to include as much information as possible in your signature. Things you can include are your full name, your job title, your phone number, relevant links such as your website or social media. Sometimes they also feature a professional photograph or a disclaimer or a privacy statement.

The last year is optional and depends on your company guidelines in the content of the email you're sending. Let's take a look at what this might look like. The purpose of your full name is self-explanatory. While your job title is important because it shows the recipient of your role in the company and level of expertise, your phone number and relevant links are included to give the recipient alternative ways of contacting you and getting more information about you and your company. The photograph is optional, but many companies include in the email signature templates that they require their employees to follow the pictures, help the receiver, better connect with the sender and see who they are.

The disclaimer, a privacy statement, is also a feature that a lot of companies use for their purely legal nature, and their purpose is to protect the employee and the company from potential legal hassles. This is why the disclaimer of privacy statements usually revolves around information security. They're designed to prevent the sharing of information from being forwarded to unknown parties. So how do you format the signature? Signatures can be simple or elaborate. Simple signatures, a basic text with each piece of information in its independent line. Here's an example of a simple signature. You've got the name, job title and contact information. Sometimes these are just plain text without any colors or branding at all.

Elaborate signatures are not written by design hinting at another level of professionalism and branding. They're often very busy and include a lot more information than what I've already listed. In addition to the name, designation, phone number, company name and photograph, these types of signatures can have the company logo and even a clickable social media icon in summary, when closing your email. You need to use both a sign off and a signature, a sign off is supposed to mark the end of the email while the signature gives the recipient information about you, the sender, your sign off can be formal, grateful, long form and contextual. Similarly, the signature can be plain text or have multiple design elements such as social media icons and your company logo.

Section Four

The most fundamental purpose of a business email is to convey a message. It doesn't matter how simple or complex the message is, the absolute minimum requirement from an email is that it gets the message across. To do this, the email needs to be easy to understand, which is the responsibility of the person writing the email. The purpose of the chapter in this Book is to guide professionals towards making their emails easier to understand and more effective communication tools when the email fails to get the message across. It's easy to blame the recipient.

The usual complaint is that the recipient doesn't understand the message. But if you study communication theory, the models of communication will teach you that while the recipient is responsible for understanding the message, the sender is also responsible for sending a message that can be understood. In other words, if someone doesn't understand the email you send, you are as responsible for that miscommunication as they are. So keep that in mind when communicating with people through email as the sender.

Your goal should be to make it as easy as possible for the receiver to understand what you're trying to say. Which naturally brings us to the next question. What does an easy to understand email look like? Essentially, three aspects determine whether the email is easy to understand or not. They are clarity, brevity and accuracy. The purpose of the entire chapter is to focus on each of these aspects in detail. Here's a brief overview of each of the chapters in the chapter and chapter one. You'll learn how to compose clear email messages. Clarity is all about comprehension in writing and emails. Clarity refers equally to the readability of the language, as it does to how well it keeps the attention of the reader.

In practice, it's all about removing ambiguity and confusion from the email. Clear email messages leave no doubt in the reader's mind about what the sender is trying to say. They prevent needless back and forth clarifications. They save time for both parties and also improve productivity. In this chapter, I will be focusing on how you can ensure that your emails are clear and easy to understand. I'll also explain the importance of knowing what you want to say in advance, understanding how your recipient thinks, and making sentences shorter. Keep your vocabulary simple and specific grammatical steps in chapter to look at writing and organizing long emails. Emails are often used for in-depth discussions and companies because they allow brainstorming over larger distances and wider time zones.

As a result, emails can get very long and complex, with complicated ideas and concepts being shared. Unfortunately, length and complexity are natural antagonists of clarity, but it is possible to make long and complex emails easier to understand so the reader can understand, digest and internalize what is being said. The secret is to manage the structure outlined in formatting of such email messages. In this chapter, I describe a very strict way to simplify and organize long and complex emails such as using subheadings lists, bullet points, fan base changes and visuals. chapter three will focus on proofreading and editing your email inconsistencies in emails, directly resulting in confusion and disorganization.

Additionally, an email containing mistakes almost always affects the reputation of the sender. So to get rid of inconsistencies or mistakes in your emails, you need to proofread and edit them in the right way. But proofreading and editing are elaborate processes that need to be handled in a structured manner to be effective. In this chapter, a focus on how professionals should proofread and edit their emails. I share how they should approach the task and what areas they should pay attention to, such as email addresses, attachments, outlines, language, facts, punctuation and spelling and chapters.

Four and five, we will look at the most common grammar and punctuation mistakes people make in business, email, communication. And in chapter six, I will share what tools you can use to quickly review your emails before you click send. If your goal is to achieve career success, you need to know how to write effectively and avoid these common errors. I share the key points you should consider when searching for grammar or tools to take a look at a number of available solutions and review their pros and cons.

It's likely that you spend a lot of time communicating with others at your job. Your written words are an extension of you, so you need to make sure that you don't look sloppy or careless in your email correspondence. After reading these chapters, you will be able to improve your writing skills and as a result, demonstrate your professionalism. There's lots of great content ahead of us. If you're ready to continue, I'll see you in the next chapter.

How to Compose Clear Email Messages

If the recipient of an email message doesn't understand what the sender is trying to say, then there's an issue with the message, but this will only happen if the email is not written. Clearly, this is why it's extremely important for there to be clarity in the email. This chapter is designed to teach professionals how to read their email messages as clearly as possible. Here's an outline of what's covered in this chapter. The importance of clarity in email messages, knowing what you want to say and to whom before writing the email, how to write shorter and simpler sentences, using nouns with pronouns to get clarity, avoiding complicated words and being specific clarities directly related to comprehension.

This means that a clear email message is easier to understand. If the recipient is unable to understand your email or loses interest halfway through, then you're not getting the most out of this wonderful tool that is IMO. On the other hand, by writing clear email messages, you will not only be ensuring that your message is understood, but also improving your chances of getting a positive response from the recipient. But what can you do to write clear email messages?

The first part of the solution is the language you use and the second part is the formatting and style. In this chapter, you learn how to perfect the language part of the solution, while in the next one you learn everything there is to know about formatting and style. If you want to achieve clarity in your email messages, the first thing you need to do is change your approach. You can no longer write your email on autopilot. You need to start thinking and become deliberate about everything you write. To do this, you need to follow three steps.

The first is try to understand your audience, try to figure out what they prioritize before figuring out what they expect from an email sent by you next. Clearly define why you're writing the email. For example, its purpose. And finally create a rough outline of what you want to see with ideas, concepts, information or instructions flowing logically from first to the last. The first step will help you empathize and get in the head of the recipient. This, in turn, will help you keep their interest. The second step will help you structure their ideas or information in your own head. This, in turn, will help you be coherent in your email, and the last step will prevent you from straying in your email message and staying focused.

It is easy to get lost in your own writing and provide information that's not really relevant in the eyes of the recipient. Longer sentences are tougher to understand because the reader is required to track multiple aspects at the same time, shorter sentences, on the other hand, are easier to understand. And do they just add quickly? Here's an example. I was reading through email and realized that the problem we face is that our resources have not been allocated properly. And here's what it looks like after simplifying the sentence.

After reading your email, I realized that resource allocation is our biggest problem. The second sentence is shorter to the point and just easier on the eyes. One of the easiest ways of shortening your sentences is to write in active form instead of passive form. Active sentences are not only shorter but also more natural. Let's see an example. A safety chapter will need to be readed by the members of this team every week. And here's what it looks like after editing it in an active voice. This team's members need to read a safety chapter every week and active sentences. The person or thing doing the action is the subject of the sentence.

In the second example, the team members are the subject of another very quick and easy way of shortening sentences is to use contractions like don't, can't, won't, shouldn't, wouldn't, and so on. While contractions help shorten sentences, the real benefit is that they make the sentence more conversational, which makes it easier to understand. Here's an example. I do not want this project to get delayed because the client would not appreciate it. And the same example after making the changes. I don't want this project to get delayed because the client would appreciate it. And the second sentence I use don't instead of do not.

When creating clear email messages, there's a rule about finishing sentences with pronouns to pronouns like this that these and those are very helpful in shortening sentences, but they don't really support clarity. This is especially true when you finish sentences with these words. Here's an example. I think I'm OK with this. You can change it to I think I'm OK with this deadline. The pronoun this in the first sentence sounds a bit ambiguous. Unless there is clearer context, the reader might not understand what you mean by this. Instead, you can replace it with a noun to clarify, as we did in the second sentence with the word deadline. Now the reader can clearly see that you're okay with the deadline.

Here's another example to illustrate this point. I don't want that to happen and supplies as it wouldn't help them. You can change this to say I don't want delays to happen and supplies as it wouldn't help the construction team. As examples show, the only way to counter the ambiguity of pronouns is to replace them with nouns. Even though this will result in your sentences getting longer, it's a small price to pay to make your sentences clearer and easier to understand in your day to day conversations, you want to use dictionary worthy words in every other sentence, even if your vocabulary is exhaustive because others may not understand what you're saying. Similarly, you will try to be as specific as possible and use simple language to help the other person understand what you're saying. But when it comes to emails, many people forget these rules.

This is why business emails often contain fancy words, vague language and technical terms. Here are some examples. The first example uses unnecessary fancy words. After commencing this fabrication project, we determined that we've not been utilizing the right equipment, resulting in delays. And here's what it looks like after making those changes, after starting this building project. We found that we've not been using the right tools, resulting in delays. The language in the second example is easier to understand, and you don't need to waste time trying to figure out what the sender is trying to say.

The next example uses vague terms. We're going to develop new consumer equipment that allows users to physically travel overlent. Instead, you can just say we're going to develop new cars. You see nice and simple examples. The final sentence is not only shorter, but also easier to understand. So in summary, when you write clear email messages, you ensure that the recipient can understand what you're saying. To do this, you need to have a clear idea of what you want to see and what your target audience is like. Along with this, you should try to shorten your sentences, back pronouns with nouns and avoid using fancy or unnecessary words.

Writing and Organizing Long Emails

Most emails are complicated and difficult to follow, this prevents the recipients from understanding the message that the sender is trying to convey. Simplifying these types of emails and making them scannable can help the recipient understand the message. The best way to do this is through the structure and outline of the email message, which means manipulating the formatting. This chapter is designed to help professionals learn various formatting tricks that will help them simplify and organize long and complicated emails.

Before we get started, let's take a look at what is covered in this chapter, how making formatting changes can make it easier to understand the importance of subheadings and how they help the right way to list things and use bullet points. Typographical modifications for emphasizing specific elements and using visuals to shorten and simplify Inose. Clarity in emails is as much about outline and structure as it is about readability and coherence of the language being used. In a way, you can say that making your language easy to understand is the first part of getting your ideas across while simplifying your email structure is the second.

The simple trick to simplifying your email, outline and structure is to make your email as scannable as possible. Making the email scannable has multiple benefits, but the foremost is that you'll be emphasizing the most important information while retaining the recipient's interests or the email. This is best done by manipulating formatting in various ways. In this chapter, we'll focus on how you can use formatting changes to make your email scannable and easier to understand, while also highlighting the most important information. An analysis from the Nielsen Norman Group on multiple studies over the years found that about 80 percent of people scan Web page text with only about 16 percent actually reading things word by word. There's a group that analyzed studies revolving around newsletters and found that people read them even more abruptly than Web pages.

While they didn't study email reading behavior, it is safe to assume that in the best case scenario, the numbers will match the general analysis, while in the worst case scenario they'll be similar to the newsletter analysis. As someone who writes business emails and wants them to be read. This means that you need to ensure your email is Erskineville. The easiest way to do this would be to start using subheadings in your emails. Subheadings offer multiple readability benefits. Here's a quick list. They break the email down into bite sized paragraphs. They convey the essential point in as few words as possible. They can be used to get the general drift of the entire message. They divide difficult and complex concepts into individual and easier to understand steps.

And five, they make it easier and quicker for the recipient to return to specific locations of the email. Let's look at a quick example of how these might look like in an email. Let's say I was writing an email explaining how to use subheadings. Here's what it would look like as one long piece of text. Instead of sending one long chunk of text, I can make it more scannable and easier to read by organizing the content and adding subheadings that looks much better at subheadings are so important that if there was only one thing you had to do while writing long and complicated emails, I would tell you to use relevant subheadings.

Listen, boys are similar to subheadings, while subheadings help break the wall of text in the entire email list, Symbolists can be used to break the constant flow of paragraphs because of their built in indentations lists. And bullies are also easier to revisit because they're easier to find. Words buried in paragraphs. Here's an example. With a series of colors, the colors can be written as the color is. We've chosen our red, yellow, blue, green, violet, purple, pink and lavender. Or they can be written as the colors we've chosen are red, yellow, blue, green, violet, purple, pink and lavender.

The second option is clear, easier to read and very easy to find. Again, in the IMO, another scenario where lists and bullets are hugely beneficial is when giving instructions or step by step procedures. The steps are understood better when provided in numbered lists. Let's see an example. Here are instructions on how to create a Gmail account. Go to www.youtube.com create an account. The sign up form will appear next. Enter your phone number to verify your account, you will receive a text message from Google with a verification code. This would be much easier to read as a numbered list. Here's how you can format it instead.

To create an account. First, go to Gmail Dot Com to create an account there. The sign up form will appear and so on and so on. These are the same instructions. But they're presented as a no list. They're easier to follow and easier in the eyes as well. Similarly, bullets are very useful. If you want to summarize chapters for the reader, for example, if you're sharing the minutes of a meeting and want to specify the highlights or findings of the discussions, you can use bullet points to make sure that the reader reads them.

Another way to emphasize specific aspects of a long and complex email is to play with typography and fonts, you'll have four options to choose from if you want to emphasize things with the typography and fonts. The first one is to italicize certain words or sentences. Italics are used to gently emphasize something. Here's an example. Please emphasize a sentence for the reader or please emphasize the sentence for the reader. As you can see, the word emphasize is italicized in the second sentence to catch the reader's attention. The second way to emphasize things is to underline the words or sentences. The intensity of emphasis with underlining is similar to italicize. In the first example let's prioritize Project A over other projects and then if you want to underline you could do it this way.

Let's prioritize Project A over other projects. In this case, Project A is emphasized. You can also build the relevant words or sentences boldly as best used when you want to emphasize something strongly. Here's an example of what that looks like. We need to start focusing on delays now so we need to start focusing on delays now with the word delays bolded to stand out from the rest of the text. The final method is to simply highlight the relevant words or sentences. While some people use this method in Ima's, it is ideally used when highlighting something within quoted text. For this reason, it is less common in business communication.

In practice, this would be used to highlight something taking out of a previously signed document like a quotation or contract. For example, Could you please clarify the refund policy mentioned in the contract? You may cancel your subscription at any time after the seven day refund period. And one of the four methods can be used to emphasize things in your email. Sometimes they can even be used interchangeably because the difference between them is very subtle. So in the end, how you emphasize your words and sentences boils down to how strong you want the emphasis to be and what your personal preferences are.

Many times words may not be enough to explain or convey concepts and ideas that are too complex in the majority of cases, this will happen when the message being conveyed has visual references. A good example would be instructions. The instructions could be for using physical equipment or even a virtual software program. In such scenarios, visual aids with notes can be very helpful in the email message. For example, for physical equipment marked up, photos can be used to convey instructions. In the case of virtual software, you can use screenshots or even GIFs to show the steps you need to convey.

Using visuals in long and complex emails can not only reduce the word count drastically, but also make your message clearer and easier to follow. In summary, the race structural and formatting focus modifications can simplify long and complex emails in a way that they become scannable and easier to understand. Subheadings less bullet points. Boulding italics underlining, highlighting and using visuals can significantly improve the coherence of your email message.

Proofreading and Editing Your Work

Before sending an email, you need to review it for consistencies and errors of various types. While inconsistencies create confusion, mistakes and an email will affect your reputation in the workplace. This is why it's so important to proofread and edit your email message before pressing the send button. This chapter focuses on the best ways of proofreading and editing your email. Here's what we're going to cover. Why proofreading and editing emails is important.

Separating writing from reviewing what to check with recipients addresses the importance of checking attachments. Why? You should check the structure of your email reviewing language, facts and punctuation and spelling and making technology work for you. The more mistakes you make when sending emails, the more unprofessional you look to the recipient. Even a single type of grammatical error can have an impact on your reputation. It isn't even about how proficient you are in writing English. It's more about how focused and aware you are when you're writing your email.

The reason for this is that even if English is not your first language, it's still possible for you to fix mistakes and errors in your email, provided you proofread and edit everything carefully. In this chapter, I will explain how you should go about proofreading and editing your emails. First, get some distance. It can be challenging to proofread and edit something you've already written. The reason for this is that when you've just written something, your mind is so familiar with the words that it starts skipping them. This is why seasoned writers and journalists almost always take a break. They take a break away from the work before proofreading and editing something.

So when you get some distance between writing and reviewing your work, your mind detaches and becomes capable of spotting mistakes again when you return. Next, look at the email addresses. The first thing you need to check on your return is the email address. You're sending the email to business. Email addresses usually start with names followed by the add sign and company names. So if your business contacts have similar names, it's very easy to enter the wrong email address in the fields. Recipient email address related errors are also more likely if you're sending the email to more than one person at a time or if you're using email templates. There are various things you need to look at here. These are first, there could be typos or unfinished email addresses, too. If you're using multiple fields such as to see CNBC, you can end up entering the email address more than once, causing confusion. Three When sending to too many people, you may be putting the email address in the two or four when it would be more appropriate to use the PCC fields to protect their privacy.

Next, you need to review attachments. It's always better to attach the files you want to send before doing anything else in the email draft. After all, it would be quite unprofessional if you talk about the attachment, but you send the email without attaching anything while you check whether you've attached the files or not. You should check them in terms of attachment. Etiquettes to the etiquettes you need to focus on are in separate chapters on attachments. But things you need to look for are whether they're attached. Files are the right ones there, file names, their sizes, they're mentioned in the body of the email and other things. Next, you'll need to reconsider the structure. It would be wise to review email from the perspective of clarity, readability and conciseness. You want to make it easier for the recipient to read your email and understand the message. Reviewing the structure of the email will help you do this.

Typically, this means looking for formatting related inconsistencies, but also including checking up on intangible things such as paragraph size flow from one paragraph to another list and bullet points. Next, you want to check the language, facts, punctuation and spelling, proofreading and editing are not complete without a detailed evaluation of the content, the biggest chunk of your time will be spent checking the content. Everything I've already mentioned early in this chapter will not take you more than just a few minutes, but this is only a small portion of the entire proofreading and editing exercise. You need to begin by reviewing the language you've used in the email. While reviewing the language, you need to check two things. These are the tone and the readability.

The tone of your email needs to match. Your relationship with the recipient, for example, could be formal, semiformal and in some rare cases, maybe even informal. When it comes to readability, you need to simplify sentences, shorten them and make it easier for the recipient to go through the email next. If you've given facts in your email, such as numbers, statistics or estimates and quotes, then you need to check them first. If you need to put numbers in fax email, then it's obvious that they're important to the message being sent. So if they're inconsistent or incorrect, then the entire message in the email can get compromised. So once you're done with the facts, you need to go back and start checking, punctuation and spelling.

Punctuation and spelling mistakes can make the email and by extension the sender look unprofessional. These kinds of mistakes usually appear when emails are written in a hurry or they're written casually or written by someone who is lacking some writing skills. Regardless of the reason, punctuation and spelling need to be checked thoroughly. Next, you'll want to use technology. Proofreading the editing can be a bit too much for most professionals to handle, especially if they're sending a lot of emails every day. While you can manually check the most important emails, you don't have to spend a lot of time on the more generic ones because you can make technology work for you.

The easiest way to do this is to put your written content in Microsoft Word and use its grammar and spelling checking tool. If you're looking for something more advanced, you can try third party apps like Family and Hemingway. While technology isn't foolproof and can never achieve the same level of accuracy as a manual review, they can speed things up considerably. Besides, they can be integrated into most email platforms as well. In summary, proofreading and editing your email is important because mistakes can make you look unprofessional and prevent the recipient from understanding what you're trying to say.

To ensure that you proofreading and editing efforts are successful, you need to start by taking a break from when you finish writing to when you start reviewing things you need to check while reviewing your email, include the recipient's email addresses, the attachments, structure of the email, language, punctuation and spelling. It might sound like a lot of things you need to remember, but once you get in the habit of checking and reviewing your emails, it'll be easier and easier every time.

Common Grammar Mistakes in Business Emails

Writing emails is an important part of business communication, the quality of your email communication can have a significant impact on how your business is perceived by others. Governance matters because when you use words correctly, you project a professional and intelligent image. However, it is very common for grammatical errors to creep into business emails.

Even with all your experience, you may sometimes not be sure if you're using the right word at the right time. With that in mind, we'll cover a list of 10 commonly made grammatical errors, along with suggestions on how to correct them. Here's what we're going to cover common grammar mistakes in business emails, how to fix these mistakes and examples to explain all of these points. First, let's look at incorrect capitalization and not capitalizing the first word in a sentence. A part of grammar that has been heavily affected by the age of instant messaging is capitalization. Some of the common capitalization errors in emails are not capitalized in the first word in a sentence or not capitalizing proper nouns such as the pronoun I.

Although capitalization rules may seem too simple to mess up, these mistakes can occur because people accidentally use the same informal grammar in emails that they use in their text messages. The best way to avoid this would be to keep these basic capitalization rules in mind while typing your emails and proofread what you've written before you present. Then there are repeated words, another common error in using the same word over and over again within a few sentences. You can start to feel tedious for the readers. You can avoid this by employing synonyms instead of the same word repeatedly.

Try not to use the same word more than twice in two consecutive sentences, if you can do without it. However, it's also important not to go too far in the opposite direction. You don't want it to seem like you're just moving down the list of suggestions in the dictionary. For example, instead of saying please update me on the project. The project deadline is approaching and the client wants to know about the progress we have made on the project. Instead, you should say, please update me on the project at the earliest. The deadline is approaching and the client wants to know about the progress we've made on it. Number three, misplaced words.

The order of your words can alter the meaning of your sentence. These errors usually occur with dangling participles, for example. These are adjectives that unintentionally modify the wrong noun in a sentence. To avoid this, check the order of the adjective to see if it conveys an accurate description. For example, we offer tea to the clients with honey and Lemon suggests that the clients brought along honey and lemons. However, we offer tea with lemons and sweetener to the clients accurately describing how the beverage was served to the clients. No, for vague words, there are a few overused and non-specific words that are commonly used in business emails.

Words such as good, nice, great, etc. can be replaced by words to describe what you're trying to say in a more concrete way, instead of just calling something nice or good. Right about why it was nice or what was good about it. For example, even a simple change, such as saying the chapter was intriguing instead of saying the chapter was great, can make a big difference. No. Five confusing homophones. A homophone is a word that's pronounced the same to varying extent as another word, but differs in meaning. These words can have distinct meanings that should not be confused in a business email.

Here are some examples of commonly misused homophones. Your versus you're your is possessive and your is a contraction of you are, for example. Your suit looks great. Means that the suit belongs to you or you're going to do this work stands for you and means that the work has been assigned to you. The next example is its versus it's, it's, it's possessive while it's with an apostrophe is a contraction of it is. For example, the dog is wagging its tail, it is possessive, the dog has a tail. It's a pleasant day. It is a contraction of it meaning the day is pleasant. Here's another common mistake people make then versus than is used to situate actions in time while then is most often used to make comparisons.

For example, we went out for lunch and then came back to work. Work came after lunch. Or here's another example. His chapter was much better than mine. We are comparing two chapters. Our next example is affect vs. effect. It is very common to make mistakes while choosing between these two words. Effect is a verb, while effect is a noun. Effect means to influence or produce a change and effect means the result or the influence. Let's look at an example. One employee's negativity can affect the whole team. What effect did the loss have on the team? Another common mistake is the wrong verb tense. This one is not technically a grammar mistake, but it is recommended that you avoid it in business emails.

It's very common to put your verbs in the past tense when you actually mean it in the present tense. For example, I wanted to discuss something with you rather than I wanted to discuss something with you. Although it's likely done not to sound too strong, it may give the impression that you're no longer interested in doing it. Here's another tip: using passive voice using passive voice isn't technically a grammar error, but you should try to limit as much as possible in your business emails. So let's look at an example. John completed the project. It's written in an active voice. The project was completed by John. That's a passive voice.

As you can see in this example, in the active voice, the subject performs the action stated by the verb. It follows a simple subject and verb and object format that's easy to read. On the other hand, in the passive voice, the subject is acted upon by the verb. This makes for a dull, indirect sentence. Therefore, writing an active voice makes your message seem more direct as it is easier to read and understand. It also sounds more energetic. Next, let's look at empty phrases. There are a few commonly used phrases that are unnecessary and end up cluttering your work email. Here are some examples of phrases that can be eliminated from your work email to make it sound more concise and straightforward.

For example, the expression. As a matter of fact, let's see it in a sentence. As a matter of fact, our sales have gone up. This can be easily replaced by our sales having gone up. Here's another example. In the process of completing the assignment, we can be replaced by we are completing the assignment. Also words such as basically, totally, literally, actually and so on. Also, don't add too much value to your message. It is important to recognize such words and phrases and reduce their use in your writing. Next, let's look at misspelled names. As you already know, building connections in business is a delicate thing and it can be easily disrupted by misspelling the recipient's name. It can leave them with a negative impression.

This mistake is usually made due to variations in the spelling of different names, cultural differences, or just maybe not paying enough attention. You can avoid this by always doing your due diligence to make sure that you have the correct spelling, being mindful of cultural differences and simply copying and pasting the recipient's name instead of having to type it manually. Next, you'll need to pay attention to misspelled words. This may seem too obvious, but according to a study done by glamorously misspelled words are the most common error.

You may misspell a word because of the speed of your typing or just because you're not sure how a word is spelled. The easiest tips for avoiding this are proofread your text and use online tools for checking grammar and spelling. In summary, if any of the mistakes we've talked about seem familiar to you and occur in your emails. It would be a good time for you to review your writing to make it more clear and accurate. Writing is a skill that can be learned and improved with practice, so writing

IMOS forms a significant part of business email communication and therefore you should make sure that you're practicing good writing habits when it comes to emails.

Common Punctuation Mistakes

You already know that email is an essential part of business communication, a crucial part of writing, a correct and easy to understand email is using punctuation accurately. Using a punctuation mark incorrectly can completely change the meaning of your sentence. This is why it's important to recognize and fix the most commonly made punctuation mistakes in email writing.

Here's what we're going to cover in this chapter. Common punctuation, mistakes in business emails, how to fix these mistakes. And we're going to look at examples that will help you understand these concepts. First, let's look at how to use apostrophes to pluralize nouns. Apostrophes are used to indicate possessions and to contract words. Apostrophes are not to be used to pluralize nouns. Here's an example. The apples were rotten here.

An apostrophe is used to pluralize the word apple, which is wrong. The apples were rotten is correct without the apostrophe. An exception from this rule is that you can use apostrophes to pluralize singular items like digits and letters. For example, fives from multiple digits or A's for multiple letters using apostrophe to show quantities without commas, sentences become long, confusing blocks of text. Here's an example. Instead, I went to the office and found out it was closed, so I went home. You should write. I went to the office and found out it was closed, so I went home to avoid this mistake. You can see the sentence out loud and notice any breaks in your speech. Add commas when you pause and when you change gears within a sentence, just like missing commas. Overusing them can also be grammatically incorrect.

A very common example of this mistake is when two main clauses are joined by a comma. For example, the office remains closed for a week. Nevertheless, the team kept up with their work. The two main clauses here are the office remains closed for a week and nevertheless the team keeps up with their work. The correct way of connecting these two clauses would be if the office remained closed for a week. Nevertheless, the team kept up with their work or the office remained closed for a week. And the sentence nevertheless comma, the team kept up with their work. Therefore, this mistake can be avoided by placing a semicolon after the first clause or by ending the first clause with a period and then starting a new sentence.

A hyphen is a small line used to connect words to create a single idea. Here's an example using hyphens. This bread is rock hard. A dash or a longer line with spaces before and after is most commonly used to indicate a meaningful pause or a quick change in thought. Here's an example. Using a dash, he's fond of two things: traveling and reading. Semicolons and Collins are often misused. You should use a in if you want to set a list of items or introduce a quote, for example, we need to buy three things: a notebook, a pen and a binder. If you want to separate two independent clauses that are directly related, meaning or subject matter, use a semicolon, for example.

I want to go on vacation. I need a break from work. You should avoid using numerous exclamation marks in business emails.

Too many exclamation marks will overwhelm the reader and devalue an individual exclamation mark. Here's an example of what to avoid. You will love working here. The team is very professional, with three exclamation marks at the end to sound professional in your writing, cut down on your use of exclamation marks and save them only for the big points or for the end of paragraphs. Avoid using single or double quotation marks where there's nothing to be quoted. Here's an example of what to avoid.

We offer the best service in town. A lot of times using quotation marks around a word suggests that the word is being used in a context other than the obvious one. Therefore, enclosing words in quotation marks merely for emphasis may confuse or annoy the reader. It's better to use a bold or italicized volunteer to emphasize a specific part of your message. We offer the best service in town. This looks much better. And a positive is a noun or noun phrase that follows another known or noun phrase and modifies it or provides additional information about it, and a positive may be essential or nonessential to the meaning of the sentence. Here's how you can determine whether a positive is essential or nonessential and a positive is essential if it narrows down the word it modifies.

Let's look at an example to clarify this point. My friend John is a doctor. Now you may have several friends, so John restricts which friend is a doctor. If we take out John from the sentence, we don't know who you're writing about. Since John is an essential or positive in this context, it does not need to be set off using commas and a positive is non essential if we know exactly who the writer is referring to, even if the positive is removed. For example, John, comma, my friend comma is a doctor in this case. We know John is a doctor, even if we don't know he's your friend. Therefore, my friend is non essential in the sentence since my friend is a nonessential appositive and is set off using commas.

Another common mistake in business emails is using a question mark at the end of a request. Here's an example. Avoid writing. Can you please send me the report as soon as possible? Question mark instead write. Can you please send me the report as soon as possible with just a period at the end. Remember that requests disguised as questions should end with a period and not a question mark. Let's look at another common punctuation mistake. This is a very commonly seen punctuation mistake in business emails if you use from use to as well. Here's an example to explain this clearly. Please read from pages 15-20.

This example is wrong. However, both please read from pages 15 to 20 and please read pages 15. 20 are correct. While it's true that some of these punctuation errors usually go unnoticed, they can quickly add up and hurt your professional image.

Even if you don't follow every punctuation rule, it is important to be aware of their existence to make the most out of your writing. So knowing how to avoid punctuation mistakes in formal business communication will help you write flawlessly. This significantly impacts how your communication skills are perceived in the long run.

Tools for Checking Grammar and Punctuation

After all the effort you put into your work, you don't want a simple grammar or spelling mistake to undermine at all. And although both Microsoft Word and Google Docs have grammar checking features built into them, they don't offer advanced grammar or style checks like these online tools. Keep in mind that this chapter will walk you through recommended tools that you can use in addition to Microsoft Word and Google Docs to check your email rating and correct your grammar and spelling mistakes. Here's what we're going to learn in this chapter.

Top five grammar checker tools, features of each one and pros and cons of each tool. The first one is primarily Grammar is a writing assistant that provides tools to help you communicate more effectively. Not only does it proofread your work and suggest corrections, it also provides an explanation for those corrections. This helps you learn from your mistakes. Grumbly has a free as well as a paid version or their premium version. While the free version helps you with spelling errors and basic grammar mistakes, the paid version catches advanced grammar and punctuation mistakes as well as contextual spelling errors.

The beat version is useful if you want to increase your knowledge of English grammar as it provides more writing insights, such as suggestions for improvement in sentence structure, word choice and readability. Let's look at the pros of using grammar. Learn first. It's easy to use because of its clean and simple user interface. It's available in multiple formats. You can use it as a Web-Based, still an extension to your Web browser and add on from Microsoft Word or even as a keyboard on your smartphone. Grimsley's free version has limited features. You will need to upgrade the grammar premium to gain access to its best features.

The second tool is called Prewriting Eight, providing aid acts as your virtual riding coach and grammar checker besides grammar. It's one of the more thorough grammar checkers online. It checks grammar, punctuation, spelling errors and style issues. And it also provides detailed feedback on your writing. Providing aid also helps you identify cliches and repeat words and phrases. You can read through the suggestions and implement what works for you. This makes for a writing aid, a great tool to improve the quality of your writing. So what are the pros? So amongst all popular grammar checkers, providing aid is one of the cheapest it offers. A lifetime subscription at a reasonable price is also available in multiple formats. It integrates with Microsoft Word and Google Docs. It's available as a desktop app for Mac and Windows, and it can also be used as a browser extension for Chrome Firefox Safari Edge to check your rating on any website.

At this time, it doesn't have a mobile app version for your smartphone. The free version limits a lot of its advanced features and allows only up to 500 words in the online tool. Another tool I wanted to mention is called Ginger. Ginger is an online tool that checks for grammar, punctuation, sentence structure and style mistakes. It also provides translation into over 40 languages like family. Ginger offers both free grammar and spelling check, as well as online proofreading software. Although the free tool is limited to 350 characters, once you sign up with Ginger, you can get a more robust Google Chrome plugin for free. This will allow you to copy and paste your text to find any errors. Ginger has a mobile app called Ginger Keyboard that can help you catch spelling mistakes and emails. It also works with Microsoft Word. The free version of Ginger is relatively more powerful. It includes three tools as an editing window with translation, a dictionary and thesaurus. It provides translations allowing you to communicate in multiple languages.

Now let's go over the concept. Ginge is not compatible with Bach or Google Docs due to the multiple steps to work through your text. Ginger slows the self editing process. You have to hover over the mistakes to find out what is wrong and then click on a text box to either accept or reject the error and that grammar. Ginger has no sidebar that lists each potential mistake. Another two are called Hemingway. Ed Hemingway. Ed is a style checker that is built to keep your writing easy to read. It highlights complex sentences and read uses of passive voice in green and excessive adverbs. And blue is up to you to fix or ignore the sentence structure. Hemingway's online app is free to use. The desktop version is inexpensive and compatible with both Windows and Mac. Let's look at the pros and cons of using this tool.

The pros are. First of all, Hemingway has a free online version. It compliments your preferred grammar and spell checker tool. And here's a list of the cons. It's not a replacement for a dedicated grammar and spell checker. It does not provide suggestions on how to edit complex sentences. You have to figure out how to fix your own text. And the last deal I wanted to suggest is called white smoke, white smoke can be used to check your writing for grammar, punctuation and spelling mistakes. It also identifies errors in sentence structure. White smoke is available in a paid version that's compatible only with your Web browser.

This version includes a grammar and plagiarism checker and a translator. White smoke premium is another version that allows you to use the app with Mac, Windows, Gmail and Microsoft Word. So what are the pros and cons? Here are the pros. Why is smoking affordable? If you don't mind paying yearly, the PEDE versions provide over 100 document templates for cover letters, grand proposals, business emails and so on. In terms of disadvantages, white smoke usually does not provide an option for monthly subscription.

You will have to upgrade to premium to get support for formats other than the Web browser. While these online grammar and spelling checker tools are a great way of enhancing your communication, they are not a replacement for common sense or the humanized. They will definitely help you cut down on errors. But you should always use your own judgment instead of relying solely on the suggestions provided by these tools. The tools mentioned in this chapter will significantly reduce the number of errors you make, and every writing is crucial for business communication.

www.ingramcontent.com/pod-product-compliance
Lightning Source LLC
Chambersburg PA
CBHW071518220526
45472CB00003B/1062